Breathe into Being

Breathe into Being

Awakening to Who You Really Are

Dennis Lewis

Theosophical Publishing House
Wheaton, Illinois * Chennai, India

Quest Books
Theosophical Publishing House
P.O. Box 270
Wheaton, IL 60187-0270

www.questbooks.net

Cover photo: Charles C. Place/gettyimages.com
Cover design by Beth Hansen-Winter

Library of Congress Cataloging-in-Publication Data

Lewis, Dennis.
Breathe into being: awakening to who you really are / Dennis Lewis—
    1st Quest edition.
    p.   cm.
ISBN 978-0-8356-0872-5
1. Breathing exercises. 2. Respiration. 3. Health. I. Title.
RA782.L488 2009
613'.192—dc22   2008051480

Printed in the United States of America

5 4 3 2 1 ★ 09 10 11 12 13 14

This book is dedicated to all my teachers,
but especially to my mother, Alyce Paxton,
who even many years after her passing continues
to be a great source of love and inspiration.

Contents

Contents

Contents

Contents

Acknowledgments

This book would not have been published without the enthusiastic support of two people: David Hykes and Richard Smoley. After reading an early, incomplete version of the book, my good friend David Hykes—award-winning composer, singer, harmonic chant pioneer, and meditation teacher—convinced me to finish the book and get it published. So I finished it and initially made it available through my website as an MS Word document. One of the people who purchased the book online was Richard Smoley, distinguished author and authority on the mystical and esoteric teachings of Western civilization. Of course, this world we live in is always full of surprises: it turned out that Richard also happened to be the acquisitions editor for Quest Books. After reading the book, Richard contacted me and asked if I would be willing to submit it for possible publication by Quest. I said yes, and the book you now have in your hands is the result.

I would like to thank my friend and colleague Mike White, the director of the Optimal Breathing School and Institute, who gave me excellent feedback on an early version of the manuscript. I would like to express my gratitude to Quest Books

Acknowledgments

editor, Sharron Dorr, whose insightful editorial suggestions and corrections helped the book immeasurably.

And finally, I would like to thank all those who have attended my talks, workshops, classes, and retreats and explored with me the miracle and mystery of breath and being.

Introduction

Welcome to *Breathe into Being*, a book that can help you awaken to who and what you really are through the miracle of the breath as it manifests now in your body.

Most books on breathing explain how and why you should work with your breath to improve your health, increase your energy, or obtain some spiritual goal—all in the future. Most books on presence explain that there is really nothing to do to be who you really are except perhaps to open your eyes right now and see that you have always been what you have been searching for.

Of course, there are books on breathing that discuss the importance of presence and books on presence that discuss the importance of breathing. There are very few (if any) contemporary books, however, that explore the depths to which breathing itself, natural breathing, is a portal to presence, an ever-present gateway to *awakening to and being who you really are.*

Breathe into Being, a natural extension of my previous books *The Tao of Natural Breathing* and *Free Your Breath, Free your Life*, has grown out of my engagement in various traditions over many years, including Taoism, Advaita, and the Gurdjieff Work—traditions whose fundamental aim is to discover and live the Truth. The book has also grown out of my personal work with breathing and presence over the past many years, as well as out of my work with individuals and groups. As such it will give you a taste of how and what I actually teach in a workshop setting.

As you read this book and undertake the practices that are given, please remember that it has been written to help you in several different ways.

A LARGER MENTAL PERSPECTIVE

First, *Breathe into Being* will help awaken in you a larger mental perspective, a perspective that will enable you to receive new, direct impressions of the truth of your life. As thinking beings, we will always have thoughts, and we will always be guided in one way or another by ideas—even if the idea we have is to free ourselves from our thoughts and ideas. A larger mental perspective is necessary because the narrow, egoistic way we think about ourselves and the world has a powerful restrictive impact on our emotions, sensations, and perceptions; and that way of thinking often keeps many of the insights and experiences we have from helping us to awaken to our real nature.

Paradoxically, those who write books about being and presence (and there are many such today) often use words to emphasize the importance of going beyond words and thoughts. But they seldom mention the fact that bigger thoughts—thoughts that include instead of exclude—create space for the miracle of being and presence to appear. Though this "little secret," as I sometimes refer to it, is seldom discussed, "big thoughts" play a major role in what happens when you attend a Satsang or other spiritual event in which you listen to the teacher speak. The presence of the teacher, along with the ideas that she or he expresses in a sincere way—ideas of self-inquiry, awakening, consciousness, love, truth, and being—resonate with a deeper dimension of yourself. They evoke an openness that allows you to go beyond your own conditioned thoughts and reactive emotions and see what you have really always known in your heart.

Conscious Contact with Your Body

Second, the book will help you come to a more direct, conscious contact with your body, not the body you take for granted and think you know so well, but your body as a sacred temple, a sacred substance of silence, through which you can return to the source of all being. The work with sensation that you will discover in this book is an engagement with the power, mystery, and energy of life itself. When you sense the various parts of your body engaged by your breath, you are learning to sense the breath of life itself. And with the overall sensation of your entire body at increasingly subtle energetic levels comes presence— *the hereness and the nowness of being.*

THE RELEASE OF PHYSICAL AND EMOTIONAL KNOTS

Third, the transformation that takes place as a result of your larger mental perspective and the living multi-dimensional sensation of your body now and here will help release the unnecessary physical and emotional knots and tensions that constrict your breath and your life. These knots and tensions, maintained in large part by your identification with past traumas and conditioning, as well as with the rigid thinking and the mental stories you tell yourself about yourself to support this thinking, sap your energy and fragment your being, and make it virtually impossible for you to experience the fullness of the breath of life.

A BENEFICIAL CHANGE IN YOUR BREATHING

And finally, your breathing itself will begin to change in a beneficial way—not because you have tried to change it but rather because you have created conditions in which your breath can flourish. The breath likes to move where there is awareness, where there is space and comfort, and where there is openness and ease of being, which the practices in this book are designed to promote. The breath is a portal to presence, and presence transforms the breath.

A Movement between Big Ideas and Living Impressions

As you work with this book you will quickly discover that there is a rhythmical movement between big ideas and questions—those that leave room for truth to manifest without resistance by the egoic mind—and the living impressions of how these ideas and questions can manifest in your own body and life. It is therefore important as you read and work with the book to take your time, ponder the ideas that are given and the questions that are asked, and try each exercise without assuming that you know what the results will or should be.

Living Impressions of Yourself as You Really Are

The exercises themselves, along with the insights and information about breathing they often include, are designed to help bring you into conscious contact with yourself, to help bring you living impressions of who you are at every level—physical, emotional, mental, and spiritual. In many cases these impressions will not be the neat and orderly impressions you hope for but will instead reveal *yourself as you are at that very moment.* Such a revelation could have to do, for example, with the mechanical quality of your thinking, the disharmony of your breathing, or a judgment you are making about yourself or someone else. And it is at the very moment such an impression appears that you may realize that what makes this impression possible is presence itself, and that this presence, this miracle of consciousness, is who you are at the deepest level. When you realize this truth, there will be no compulsion to *react* to what you see, though you will no doubt *respond* in an appropriate way.

Learning to Use Conscious Experience and Inner Sincerity as a Guide

Each chapter of this book contains a specific practice, whether it is a practice of pondering or questioning or experimenting with your breath. In many cases I have not suggested how long you should work with each chapter or practice. Such suggestions, while seemingly helpful, can sometimes be a great disservice to you, the reader, since only you can know what you are experiencing at any moment and when you are ready to move on. What this book asks you to do is to use your own conscious experience and inner sincerity as a guide. When you truly feel that the meaning of the chapter has opened for you, feel free to proceed to the next chapter. As you continue working in this way, you may also find yourself called from inside to return to earlier chapters where new meanings may suddenly reveal themselves.

PRACTICING IN THE MIDST OF LIFE

In many cases, I suggest that you also try the practices throughout the day along with whatever else you are doing. This is important. It is one thing to get a sense of the practice as you are reading the book; it is quite another to allow the practice to begin to come alive when you need it most—in the thick of the movements and situations and turmoil of your everyday life. For it is in the habitual flux, confusion, and patterns of our so-called ordinary life that we fall asleep most easily and lose sight of who we really are. But it is also our ordinary life that provides the frequent shocks that can help us awaken from our illusions and dreams.

EACH CHAPTER IS A MENTAL, PHYSICAL, OR EMOTIONAL PORTAL TO PRESENCE

As you will see, most of the chapters are short, but don't let their length mislead you. In addition to raising important questions or providing useful information, each chapter is a mental, physical, or emotional portal to being, a doorway into who or what you really are. Even when you are working with a small part of yourself—your eyes, for example— the deep sensation that arises as a result of this work can guide you into the unknown miracle of yourself. The key is simply to be present, to pay attention without any expectation or judgment, to what is happening as you read and practice and live. And it is to realize that *being* this presence, along with whatever appears within its field of illumination, is the very miracle and meaning for which you have been searching.

The Mystery of Ourselves

You are about to begin on a new journey into yourself. Before starting on a new journey it is always helpful to know where you already are. So take a few minutes here to ponder your entire life up to now. See if you can *remember* everything about yourself and your life all at once—including the smells, sensations, sounds, sights, thoughts, feelings, fears, hopes, questions, insights, sorrows, joys, pains, pleasures, frowns, smiles, faces, relationships, and so on. Please stop reading at the end of this sentence, close your eyes, and simply welcome all the experiences of your life into your awareness now.

Whenever we really pause for a moment and look, we see that we are faced with the mystery and miracle of ourselves here and now as living, breathing beings. Whatever scientific, religious, and spiritual beliefs we may have about this mystery, when we are honest with ourselves we realize that we are often "asleep" to its unfathomable immediacy, its "now-ness."

Of course, we see many other things as well. We see that we move through our lives in a state of waking sleep, a state of psychological, cultural, and spiritual hypnosis. Instead of being present to the great miracle of ourselves as breathing beings and to the limitless expanse of awareness that underlies our existence, we stake out narrow, limited territories based on our personal self-image, an image constructed through many years of conditioning by society, family, teachers, friends, media, and all the forces of modern life vying for our attention. This self-image, which we quickly learn to objectify and call "I," is closely tied in with our religious and spiritual beliefs, our ideas of right and wrong, our judgments and expectations, our hopes and fears, and our likes and dislikes.

Since the very act of staking out these territories is one of separation not only from others but from the essential mystery of our own inner being, we seldom notice the various ways in which we create misunderstandings and violence both in and around us. Instead of being aware of and dealing with our own confusion, anxiety, assumptions, traumas, and lack of awareness and harmony, we often project these traits outside of ourselves and become caught up with our opinions about how other people, groups, institutions, nations, and cultures should change to reflect our ideals and desires. Instead of seeing and welcoming the world as it is, we generally either reject *what is* in favor of what we believe *should be*; or we entangle it so deeply in our own self-serving stories that *what actually is* remains hidden from us at the deepest levels. Instead of awakening to the boundless awareness of I AM, the boundless being that we fundamentally are, we live imprisoned in our own little territories, not realizing that real freedom is just a breath away—the breath that is occurring at this very moment, the breath of presence.

More than ever, awakening to "who we really are" is important not just for ourselves but for society and the world. It is quite clear that we cannot solve the problems we face today with the very same unconscious, manipulative mind that created them in the first place. Yet that is what many of us are trying to do much of the time. No matter what political beliefs, psychologies, healing modalities, breathing modalities, spiritual approaches, or ways of living we subscribe to, we are all slaves to the little territories we have staked out to support our self-image. Or we become enslaved in the name of some kind of progress, whether it has to do with social or political progress, healing, consciousness, spiritual understanding, or whatever. And our identification with and attachment to these tiny territories of belief and perception ultimately create unnecessary confusion and suffering not just for ourselves but for all those with whom we come in contact.

With awakening, however, comes a radical new understanding. This is not just the understanding that the immensity of Truth can never be comprehended by the mind; it is also the understanding that beneath the unique colors and fragrances and forms and conditions of our manifestations on this earth, however good or bad we may judge them to be, we are all the same in our deepest nature. Presence *is* what we are, when we are truly ourselves. The term "self-realization" comes close to conveying this understanding, though it may be helpful to remind ourselves that it is not a matter of knowing something deeper about ourselves but rather of experiencing the mystery of ourselves as completely unknown—the miracle of *awakeness* itself.

The breath of life flows most fully through us when we are free from the known and are living instead from the unknown in ourselves. What is curious, indeed startling, is that the more intimate we become with the sensations, feelings, and thoughts that reside within our consciousness—no matter how difficult or wonderful we might think them to be—the freer and more loving and more conscious we discover ourselves to be in our living presence.

So why not pay attention to your breath right now? Ask yourself from where it comes and to where it returns. You can also ask this question next time you are with a loved one or friend or enemy or just by yourself. You can check in on your breathing any time at all, since *you are always being breathed now*, and ponder for a moment this essential miracle of yourself, the miracle of being itself breathing.

A Sense of Infinite Potential

Our first action on this earth was to open ourselves to the breath of life, and our breath has long since been our ever-present companion. As young children, most of us experienced this breath of life directly in our bodies and feelings as a sense of infinite potential. Living as we did in the vast expanse of the present moment, where time itself seemed infinite, we experienced life as a wondrous, unknown mystery and felt that nearly anything was possible. We felt ourselves as pure receptivity and welcoming, filled with magical impressions of bodily movements, sounds, touch, sensations, smells, feelings, and thoughts.

As we grew up under the guiding hands of our parents and educators, however—people who themselves were conditioned and shaped by the particular familial and societal conditions in which they in turn had grown up—many of us began to lose our sense of wonder. We learned to define ourselves and the world in ways that allowed us to live as much as possible in a *known* world we began to take for granted, a world bound by laws and rules that defined our place and possibilities. We began to see ourselves more or less as others saw us, as external objects changing with time, and we defined ourselves in relation to what we saw, instead of what we sensed and felt in our inner world.

13

The breath of presence that awakened our bodies and hearts as young children gradually became a pale reflection of itself.

Can you remember now the sense of infinite potential that you felt at special moments during childhood? Take a moment and see if you can remember the wondrous breath of presence, of life, as it moved through you then. It may come in the form of an expansive sensation, a smell, a feeling, a thought—right now. Don't try to do anything with this experience; just allow it to touch the whole of yourself.

Working with Your Breath Begins with Awareness

Whatever we may have experienced as young children, we are faced with ourselves *as we are* today. But what or who are we really? Who are you? Are you in your essence now any different than you were as a young child? Are you the object you see so often in the mirror about two or three feet in front of you, the object that ages with time and has graying hair, wrinkles, sagging skin, or other such changes to prove it? Or are you the unchanging sense of I AM, the inner witness who experiences these impressions? Or are you perhaps in some mysterious way both and neither? I am sure you have had the experience of standing in front of a mirror and realizing that the image staring back at you from some distance has little to do with the experience you have of yourself from *no distance*, where you are fully and immediately present to yourself.

Take a moment now to stand in front of a mirror or, if there is no mirror nearby, imagine you are standing there. As you examine the one-dimensional features of the body reflected there, allow your attention to move inside toward the internal, multidimensional spaces of your own being, toward the breath of presence that fills your inner world, toward who or what is actually looking. See if you can stay in touch with the outer image in the mirror and your inner being simultaneously. Perhaps you begin to feel the question "Who am I?" in a new way.

Check in on Your Breathing

One way to begin to explore the question "Who am I?" more deeply is to allow your awareness to move inward with your breath, to experience yourself as a *breathing being*. The process of breathing is a living metaphor for understanding how to expand your narrow, restrictive sense of yourself and be present to the miraculous energies of life that are both in and around you. As a manifestation of the breath of life, every breath you take both reflects and shapes who you are at that moment.

So check in on your breathing right now. Allow all the sensations of your breath—all the internal and external movements related to how you are breathing now—to enter your awareness. See if you can discern what parts of your body your breathing engages. Just be aware of what your breath feels like and how this awareness influences your sensation of yourself. How do you feel? What, if any, new perceptions have appeared? Without coming to any conclusions, what does this experience and what do these perceptions tell you about who you are?

Check in on your breathing as many times as you can throughout your day. A minute or two at a time is enough. This simple action will begin to activate your inner awareness, your inner presence.

Our Breath Connects Us with All of Life

Every time we inhale, we breathe in 10^{22} atoms, including approximately one million of the same atoms of air inhaled by everyone who has ever lived on this planet. Every time we exhale, we return these atoms to the atmosphere to be renewed not just for those living on the earth right now but also for all future generations. Just being aware of these simple facts can have a profound impact on your breath and on your sense of yourself.

Keeping these facts in mind, can you stay in touch consciously with both your inhalation and your exhalation now without trying to change them in any way? Can you experience yourself as a being somehow connected through your breath with everyone who has ever lived or who will ever live on the earth? Allow yourself *to feel* the implications of this amazing fact.

Many of us live as though we are separate entities. Yet our breathing clearly tells us otherwise. Not only do we breathe many of the same atoms of air breathed in by everyone who has ever lived on this planet, but every time we inhale we take in oxygen previously expelled into the atmosphere as a so-called waste product by the earth's myriad plant life. Every time we exhale, we expel carbon dioxide as a so-called waste product into the atmosphere where it can eventually be utilized by this same plant life. When we look, we see that everything in nature is connected with everything else and that nothing is wasted. We see that our breath is a link in the cosmic ecology—in the conservation, transformation, and exchange of substances in nature's intricate metabolism.

Allowing your attention to move inward as you follow your inhalations and exhalations, can you sense some kind of energy exchange taking place in your body right now with each breath that you take? Can you begin to feel yourself as part of something very large, something that your thoughts cannot really comprehend?

Our Breath Connects Our Inner and Outer Worlds

When we allow our attention to move inward, we see that our breath connects our inner world of thoughts, feelings, and sensations with the enormous scale of the outer world—including the earth and its atmosphere, as well as all organic life—through the continual and perceptible alternation of yin and yang, contraction and expansion, emptying and filling. If we can consciously experience it in the larger context of the whole of life, the process of breathing shows us how to let go of the old and open to the new. It offers an intimate pathway into ourselves, into the realization of who and what we really are.

This realization begins with the living sensation of ourselves now and here as breathing beings. Check in on your breathing now. What do you sense? Can you sense this process of opening and closing, filling and emptying, as it takes place at this moment in your body? Can you sense the air coming in from the outside world through your nose and into your body and then being returned to the outside world again? What does it feel like simply to be present to your breath?

The Freedom of Simple Presence

When you check in on your breathing innocently, without any motive or effort to change it, you free yourself, at least momentarily, from your self-image, from those thoughts and reactive emotions that create so many of the problems in your life. As you check in on your breathing again and again you will begin to reside more often in the miraculous freedom of presence, the freedom underlying all the so-called problems and complexities of what you take to be yourself and your life.

Try it now while reading and pondering these words. Check in on your breathing. Simply sense what happens in your body as the breath of life moves through it. As you do so you may notice the arising of impatience and anticipation. Thoughts and emotions may arise saying you need or want to do something differently, anticipate what will be said next, take care of some important issues, and so on. Invariably, no matter what words you use to describe them, these thoughts and emotions will generally be about changing what you are feeling right now, escaping discomfort or boredom, or doing something you believe will improve your life. You may also notice that you don't always have to believe in your thoughts and emotions; indeed, being present to them frees you from any need to react at all.

We Can Only Find Meaning and Happiness Now and Here

For most of us in today's future-driven world, our attention is almost always focused outwardly. Our attention is directed toward obtaining in the future those things or objects or experiences that we believe will give our lives meaning or make us happy. The present moment, where we are right now, is viewed as a mere transition to some better time and place or as an obstacle to our happiness. Many of us have not yet understood that though future-oriented goals are absolutely necessary for intelligent living, the only time and place we can ever find the meaning or happiness that we know is our birthright is right now and right here. For it is now and here that the breath of life flows through us and offers us, if we can be present to it, its rich impressions and energies in a closer, more intimate relationship with ourselves and others.

Can you be content to relate to and experience yourself right now and right here as a breathing being, with nowhere else to go and nothing else to do? Give yourself at least five minutes to explore this question. Notice what arises in your thoughts and feelings. To give this practice even more substance, try the same thing with the next person with whom you come in contact. Just be fully present with that person as though there were no other place or time to be—for at this moment there really isn't. As you do so, check in on your breathing.

Learning to Live in the Present Moment

Of course, we all give lip service to living in the present moment, but in a culture that conditions us to never-ending future progress this is far easier said than done. I am not suggesting we shouldn't think about and make intelligent plans for the future—that would be not only impractical but also foolish. What I am suggesting is that we need to find a way of living in which our thoughts about and plans for the future take place in a field of presence that keeps us rooted to the only time and place we can ever live—now and here.

A simple practice you can undertake is to spend at least twenty minutes a day consciously allowing things to be exactly the way they are, no matter what you are doing and no matter what resistance may arise. The first several times you try this practice, it might be helpful to do it in quiet circumstances, where there will be a minimum of external distractions.

Once you are able to practice in quiet circumstances for twenty minutes, try allowing things to be exactly as they are for at least five minutes at a time when you are with others. This will undoubtedly be more difficult. Just remember to check in on your breathing. This will help anchor you in the present moment.

As you try these simple, natural practices, notice the kinds of thoughts that appear and see how they impact your breathing, your emotions, and the tensions in your body. As you work with this practice over several weeks you will begin to notice, often quite spontaneously at other times of the day, how your thoughts about the future frequently take you out of the present moment. They can make it difficult to see and appreciate what is actually going on in your own mind and body as well as in your so-called external environment. This practice of allowing, in full awareness and without judgment, things to be exactly as they are will transform your relationship not only with yourself and others but also with your entire life.

What Do You Really Want?

It may seem like a paradox to talk about allowing things "to be exactly as they are" at the same time we talk about transformation. But the fact is that not only do we generally not actually see what is staring us right in the face, but when we do, we run from our perception *of how things are now* to some image or expectation or idea of how things *should be in the future*. And this process takes place quite mechanically, almost as if there were no other possibility. So when I use the word transformation, I am referring to learning how to receive what is happening now in a new, more impartial way, without any judgment or analysis. This is a transformation of the very way we register our perceptions to ourselves.

Of course, not all of us want to go through this process of transformation. Many of us are quite content to live with our beliefs and our ways of viewing ourselves and the world. So here, before we go on, I suggest you take some time to look into your heart and mind and ponder what it is that, beneath all your fleeting desires, you really want. A big help in this process would be to put it into words and write these words down. After you have written them down, it may be helpful to put one hand on your belly and the other on your heart and follow your breathing for a few minutes, letting yourself become one with it. Then look closely at the words again and see if they resonate with what you actually feel. Are the words true? Is what you wrote down what you really want? What do you really want? Try writing what you really want again in a more honest way.

The Longing for Relationship

At the core of each of us—no matter what our political and social and spiritual beliefs—is a longing for real relationship, with ourselves, with others, and perhaps even with God. In other words, what many of us really want is a relationship with Truth. Though it is clear that a real relationship requires both giving and receiving, what is not so clear to many of us is that giving usually comes first. Imagine trying to take a full free breath without having exhaled fully. It's not possible. And yet that is how many of us often breathe and live our lives. We often try to fill ourselves with breath, with chi, with prana, with energy (no matter what we call it), as well as with the physical, emotional, mental, and spiritual objects of our desire, without first emptying ourselves and creating space by letting go, by giving up what is no longer necessary, or simply by giving from the heart.

We will explore the importance of a full exhalation in more depth later. For now, ask yourself these questions: How would the breath of life manifest in me if I never fully exhaled? Who would I be if I were unable to give up my old thoughts, attitudes, and beliefs? Really ponder these questions as honestly as you can.

Following Your Inhalation and Exhalation

To begin exploring the breath of life and its relationship to giving and receiving, and to who we really are and what we really want, one of the simplest, safest, and most revealing practices you can undertake is consciously to follow your breathing in the many circumstances of your day.

Try it now. As you inhale through your nose, simply be aware that you are inhaling. As you exhale through your nose, simply be aware that you are exhaling. For the moment, see if you can remain free from your judgmental mind, sometimes called "the monkey mind," the mind that disconnects you from both yourself and others. Make no judgments about how you are breathing. Just be aware of inhaling and exhaling through your nose. Try it for several breaths. See what it feels like just to put your attention completely on exhaling and inhaling. Be sincere with yourself about what you see. There is nothing else to do now except be in conscious relationship with your breath.

Being Inspired and Expired

What actually happens as we breathe? As inhalation occurs, we are filled from what we call the outer world with life-giving substances—not just with oxygen and other gases, but also with the spiritual energies within the breath, the energies of chi, prana, and so on. It is as though life itself, in its infinite variety, pours into us and fills us with new perceptions and impressions that resonate in some deep way with what is already present. We are inspired. As exhalation occurs, we let go of everything that is no longer necessary to us—the excess carbon dioxide and other gases—and return them to what we call the outer world, where they can be utilized by other living things. We are expired. There is no doing here, just following, listening, awareness, and appreciation as your breath moves in and out through your nose.

Staying in whatever physical position you find yourself right now, can you sense something of this process of exhaling and inhaling, giving and receiving, in yourself? Give yourself as much time as you need. There is nothing to accomplish. All that is being asked is that you experience this already occurring process in yourself.

The Importance of Breathing through Your Nose

Please note that I asked you for the preceding practice to inhale and exhale through your nose. In your daily life, it is important, when possible, to breathe only through your nose. There are many physical, emotional, and metaphysical reasons for this. We shall discuss just a few of them here.

First, the hairs that line our nostrils filter out particles of dust and dirt that can be injurious to our lungs, and the mucous membranes of the septum, which divides the nose into two cavities, further prepare the air for our lungs by warming and humidifying it.

Second, breathing through the nose helps maintain the correct balance of oxygen and carbon dioxide in our blood. When we breathe through the mouth, which is much larger than the nose, we usually inhale and exhale air quickly in large volumes. This often leads to overbreathing, or breathing excessively fast for the actual conditions in which we find ourselves, which influences not only our physical health but also our emotional health.

And third, when you breathe through your nostrils the air stimulates the olfactory nerves and thus your brain. This helps your brain maintain its natural rhythms, which is one of the conditions needed to support full consciousness.

Check your breathing now. Are you breathing through your nose? Check in frequently during the rest of the day to make sure you are doing so.

Breathing and Walking

Now you're going to experiment with being aware of your breathing during movement, which, of course, makes up a large part of your life. While breathing in and out through your nose, get up and walk around for fifteen minutes, observing and sensing your breathing as you walk. Notice how your breath responds to each step you take.

The way you walk is closely related to your breathing and your emotional state. By sensing your breathing as you walk, you will get new, more intimate insights, not just into your breathing, but also into your current emotional state.

First, walk for at least five minutes in whatever way seems appropriate to you. How does your breathing feel? What emotions do you experience?

Now experiment with the way you walk. Slow down, speed up, take longer or shorter strides, swing your arms in different ways, and so on, and see how this influences your breath and emotions. What you may eventually discover is that walking with awareness (whether you are in a hurry or not) promotes the fluidity and spaciousness of your breath and will thus help you find a state of dynamic relaxation and presence. At the very least it will help stimulate and harmonize your breathing.

Carbon Dioxide Regulates Our Breathing

We talked earlier about how "overbreathing" can influence our health and well-being. It is important to understand that it is the amount of carbon dioxide in our blood that generally regulates our breathing. Exhaling too much carbon dioxide too quickly is easy to do when we breathe through our mouths, which often happens when we are anxious, talk too rapidly, walk quickly, or run. At such times the arteries and vessels carrying blood to our cells constrict. In addition, the red blood cells get "sticky" and hold on to the oxygen in the blood. In such cases, we may have plenty of oxygen in our lungs and blood, but the oxygen in our blood may be unable to reach the cells of the brain and body in sufficient quantity. The lack of sufficient oxygen going to the cells can turn on our sympathetic nervous system, especially its fight or flight or freeze response, and make us tense, anxious, irritable, and even depressed. Some researchers believe that chronic mouth breathing and the associated hyperventilation it brings about can result in asthma, high blood pressure, heart disease, and many other medical problems.

To see what mouth breathing feels like, take fast deep breaths in and out through your mouth right now for thirty seconds (do not try this if you have high blood pressure or any other major illness). How does that make you feel? Then just allow your breathing to proceed quietly through your nose, and continue breathing this way if possible. Note the different sensations you experience during these very different modes of breathing.

The World of Sensation

The world of sensation is a world of great power and mystery, a world filled with the potential for rich, informative perceptions and impressions of different kinds. Most of us, however, make little use of this potential. To be sure, we take in many impressions through our external senses of seeing, hearing, tasting, smelling, and touching.

But there is another aspect of the world of sensation with which many of us have little conscious experience. This is the world of kinesthetic and organic sensations, the sensations that put us in touch with the inner dimensions of our own bodies and the thoughts and emotions that shape them. Because we are often more attracted to impressions coming from the so-called outside world, and to the thoughts and feelings that arise in relation to them, we generally take these internal bodily sensations for granted. We pay attention to them only when we have an intense physical experience of some kind—pleasure, pain, discomfort, and so on. This is unfortunate, because these internal sensations are constantly speaking to us, constantly telling us about our relationship to ourselves, others, and our environment. And, perhaps even more importantly, these sensations offer us a passageway into presence and to the sense of who we really are.

Check in on your body right now. What do you sense? Check your face, neck, shoulders, arms, hands, chest, back, belly, pelvis, legs, and feet. Take your time. Notice the various areas of tension and relaxation in the different parts of your body. Let your awareness go inside your body into your bones, fluids, and organs. See if you can have a sensation of your entire body all at once. When you have begun to sense your entire body to some extent, feel free to move on to the next section.

Densities of Sensation

When we reflect on the meaning of sensation, most of us think about it in more or less one-dimensional terms. "Sensation is sensation," we say to ourselves. "It feels good, it feels bad, or it feels neutral." For those of us interested in real presence, however, the picture changes dramatically. As we begin to sense ourselves more intimately, we discover that our internal sensations have many different densities and levels. We learn that these densities and levels often correspond to the underlying densities and levels of life and consciousness themselves. We can discern, for example, solid, earth-like sensations; liquid, water-like sensations; and gaseous, air-like sensations. We can experience the dense, ice-like contracted sensation of pain; the fluid, water-like sensation of pleasure; and the gas-like, spacious sensation of joy and love.

As we go deeper into who or what we really are, we will begin to experience the "empty," open sensation of inner spaciousness and freedom, the spaciousness and freedom that lies behind and around the thoughts, emotions, beliefs, judgments, and expectations that make up our self-image. Here we experience ourselves as pure opening, pure welcoming, and pure receptivity.

Sense your body and breath now. For the next few minutes, see if you can differentiate areas of sensation that feel dense, fluid, or spacious. Just be aware of the different densities or frequencies within. Don't analyze or judge what you experience. Just allow the different densities to be there simultaneously in your awareness.

Finding a Comfortable, Erect Sitting Posture

Now, you're going to go a bit deeper within your body to explore your breath more fully. To go deeper, however, it is important to find a comfortable yet stable and erect sitting position. This position will help release any unnecessary tensions in your muscles and help ensure that you don't generate new ones.

Here, it may be necessary to give up any ideas you may have about the "proper" meditative sitting position and simply be honest with yourself. Sitting cross-legged on the floor or on a cushion is great for people who are able to do so easily and comfortably, but for those people whose back, pelvic, hip, or leg muscles feel tight in this position (which includes most Westerners), it would probably not be appropriate, since tight muscles can inhibit taking a full, natural breath. What's more, the tension and pain that this position often produces for those not accustomed to it can distract your attention and make it more difficult to be present to the whole of yourself. So if you feel uncomfortable in a cross-legged position, it may be better to sit in a firm chair, with your feet flat on the ground.

Whatever posture you choose, it is important to keep your spine as erect as possible without impeding its movement in any way. Unless you have a back injury of some kind, therefore, it is best not to lean against the back of the chair, since doing so will put pressure on your spine and ultimately impede the full movement of your diaphragm. Be aware of your breathing for several breaths as you take your time and experiment with different sitting positions, rocking forward and backward and from side to side on your buttocks (especially on your sit bones) until you find a truly comfortable, erect posture.

Going Deeper through the Sensation of Your Breath

In this position, as you inhale and are aware that you are inhaling, sense the air going from the tip of your nose, back through your nose and throat, down into your trachea, and finally into your lungs. As you exhale and are aware that you are exhaling, sense the air going from your lungs, up through your trachea and throat, and out through your nose. Take your time.

Pay attention to how the air feels as it touches all the tissues on its way into and out of your lungs. You may notice what can be sensed as energetic, almost "electrical" charges or exchanges taking place between the incoming and outgoing air and the tissue of your nose, throat, trachea, and lungs. If you sense these exchanges, just enjoy them and treat them as nothing special. If you don't sense them now, that's okay too; you will eventually. The main thing is to be present to what is actually happening without any attempt to visualize or achieve a specific result. Work in this way for several breaths before moving on to the next chapter.

Becoming Free from Your Automatic Thoughts and Emotional Reactions

Now simply follow your breathing in the simplest way you can. As you inhale, realize that you are inhaling. As you exhale, realize that you are exhaling. Focusing your mind on what is happening inside yourself as you breathe, including all the sensations that are arising, will help free you from your automatic thoughts and emotional reactions and thus enable you to wake up in your daily life more often, to live with more receptivity and clarity in the present moment. You may find this practice especially useful at moments when you are anxious or angry. With roots in Buddhism and the other great spiritual traditions, it is a wonderful practice for everyone. So try it as often as you can remember throughout the day.

Do Less and Listen More

As you work with your breath in the way just described, be sure to check yourself before, during, and after you practice. Sense your entire body as you work and note any subtle feelings and thoughts that arise. Notice if your effort to be aware of your inhalations and exhalations is producing unnecessary tension in your body or mind.

Unfortunately, many of us are so accustomed to excessive tension in just about everything we do that we don't even realize that we are tense or that we are working in a tense way. This tension often comes from our minds, our thoughts, or our desire for change. There is a kind of underlying attitude that, without willfulness and tension, results are not possible. We need to observe this attitude in action in ourselves and see how it interferes not only with our breathing but also with the real joy of being alive on this earth.

If you observe excessive tension in your body as you work, perhaps you are working with too much effort. If your awareness tells you this is true, simply do less and sense and listen more. See if you can discover the meaning of the expression "an effortless effort." Imagine that you are a bird watcher, and that the slightest sound or movement will change the patterns and movements of the birds you are watching and give you false information about their natural activities away from humans. Try it now. Follow your breathing again, only this time see if you can follow it not from your ego or will or thoughts but from some quiet, unknown place in yourself. See if you can discover the true meaning of an "effortless effort."

Contradictory Motivations

Don't become discouraged if the meaning of "effortless effort" seems difficult to experience at first. A person very close to me complained about how often she had to take her car in to the garage to get the brakes repaired. I drove with her and noticed that she often kept one foot lightly on the brake pedal as the car was moving and sometimes even as she pressed down on the gas pedal. Now I am no genius, especially when it comes to automobiles, but I knew that this habit had to be contributing to the brake problem, a point also made by one of the mechanics to whom she took the car for repairs. There was nothing intrinsically wrong with the car, but there was certainly an issue with the driver's often pressing on the gas pedal and the brake pedal at the same time. There were, as one might say, "contradictory motivations."

Many of us go through life this way, with one foot on the brake pedal and one on the gas, and this practice can cause many so-called problems in our life. If you are making a simple effort of attention to follow your breath, but your mind, habits, stress, fear, or anxiety tell you to control it in some way, an "effortless effort" won't likely occur. Following your breath will be difficult if you are unconsciously caught up in thoughts, attitudes, and emotions that try to clamp down on your breathing in order to see and feel less of the truth, of what is really occurring. Yet this is where many of us are today, unwilling to look at our real motivations for what we do.

This problem of contradictory motivations is not just important in learning how to follow your breathing, it is also crucial in just about every aspect of living. I would like to suggest for anyone who is interested that you begin to check in on your actual motivations for whatever you are doing, especially when you seem to be experiencing anxiety, fear, anticipation, or stress. You can start with simple awareness of your breathing. Just notice what parts of your body are engaged. Then allow your attention to go a bit deeper, especially into the area of your solar plexus, belly, and back. Do you feel any tightness or holding in these places? If so, allow your attention to shine light on your thoughts. What are you thinking about, and what subtle emotions seem to be arising from these thoughts? It has been said that "the truth shall set you free," and it is my experience that this is so. It may even resolve many of what you call your personal problems, since these problems are often the result of how we think about ourselves and our lives. The problem is that we all have a vested interest in what we think the truth should be. So be sincere about what you see. Reasons may exist for hiding from others, but you seldom have a good reason for hiding from yourself.

If in following your breath you notice that you are breathing in a superficial way and holding your breath a lot, there is a reason. And only you—through your own inner awareness and sincerity—can see what this reason is. With impartial seeing often comes freedom and a new, fuller experience of the breath of life. To be sure, this work with sensing our frequently contradictory motivations may take time, and it may even require the help of those with more expertise to uncover what is really going on in us, but it is well worth it.

Self-Sensing and the Breath

Opening to the sensations of the body, which I often refer to as *self-sensing*, brings us into a more genuine relationship with ourselves, since it reveals how we actually respond to the inner and outer circumstances facing us. It also has a beneficial impact on our nervous system, helping to bring about the natural changes necessary for harmonious functioning and development. The human brain includes some 100 billion neurons, each of which "touches" some 10,000 other neurons. These neurons have many functions, but one of the main ones is to connect the various parts of the organism with one other, so that the organism as a whole can function in an integrated way while carrying out its activities. Through self-sensing we provide the organism with information it might not otherwise receive. We begin to learn firsthand about the interrelationships of our breathing, thoughts, emotions, postures, and movements. By noticing the sensations of our body, especially our breathing, in both the quiet and not-so-quiet circumstances of our lives, we experience connections between dimensions of ourselves that ordinarily escape our awareness. Self-sensing gives our brain and nervous system the spacious perspective it needs to help free us from our habitual psychophysical patterns of action and reaction. It helps free us from our various identifications and attachments with some function or manifestation of ourselves. When we pay *choiceless* attention to what is, we become one with awareness, with presence.

Try it now for a minute or two. Whatever position you are in, sense your entire body, including your breathing. Become innocently intimate with all the sensations that are occurring, opening as much as possible to them. Also include the shapes and energies of the thoughts and feelings that are taking place— negative or positive, it doesn't matter. Don't attempt to change anything. Simply get as close as possible to everything that is happening. Notice how allowing yourself to get closer to what is actually happening in your own body and mind seems to open up a much more spacious sensation of yourself, a sensation of "wholeness."

Breathing Inside the Sensation of Yourself

Now, without losing the sensation of wholeness, find a comfortable, erect sitting posture. On the in-breath, be aware that you are inhaling; sense the air going from the tip of your nose, back through your nose and throat, down into your trachea, and finally into your lungs. On the out-breath, be aware that you are exhaling; sense the air going from your lungs, up through your trachea and throat, and out through your nose. Take your time. Be sure to stay in contact with the entire sensation of your body; notice how the air feels as it touches all the tissues on its way into and out of your lungs. Notice also whatever thoughts or feelings are present. The main thing is to be present to what is happening inside this overall sensation.

Following Your Breath into Silence

As you begin to pay close attention to the sensations of the breath as it moves through the whole of yourself, you are called to move inward, toward the source, the wellspring, of your life. As you do so, you will experience a profound sense of stillness, of silence, underlying not only your breath but also your thoughts, feelings, and sensations. In short, you are called home to another, more fundamental dimension of yourself. If you can hear this call and don't resist it, you may discover that you are spontaneously freed from many of the unnecessary mental, emotional, and physical tensions keeping you imprisoned in your narrow self-image and the constricted, impoverished breathing it fosters. You begin to open to and welcome the incredible miracle of aliveness itself. Through this opening and welcoming, your breathing is freed up and your thoughts, feelings, and actions take on new intelligence and meaning. You begin to live your life rooted in the deep, silent reality that connects us all and makes us one family.

So try the "Breathing Inside the Sensation of Yourself" practice again. This time, sense how your breath moves into and out of the deep silence that underlies all your experience.

Sensing the Welcoming Presence

When we experience our breath at the deepest levels in ourselves, we are experiencing our own deepest identity. In the Old Testament we find, "And the Lord God formed man of the dust of the ground and breathed into his nostrils the breath of life; and man became a living soul" (Gen 2:7). In all the spiritual traditions we find chants, mantras, and sounds to bring us back into attunement with the cosmic symphony, a symphony in which each one of us is a note consisting of many harmonics.

Our breath, if we can but follow it inward as it flows through us in its many forms, beckons us toward the miracle and mystery of the silent, creative source of all life, the *welcoming presence* that we can sense when we look quietly within. Can you sense this presence now? Close your eyes and take a few minutes to experience this welcoming presence, this inner vibrant space and silence that includes within it everything that is happening without conflict.

What Was Your Original Face?

When we turn our attention backward or inward toward this welcoming presence, this mostly unknown dimension of ourselves, we touch again that sense of infinite potential that most of us felt as children, a sense that something miraculous is possible at this very moment. In fact, the awareness of the sensation itself *is* the miracle. We find this turning of our attention toward our innermost being in all the great spiritual traditions. In Zen, this turning of our attention is uniquely captured in the koan that goes something like, "What was your original face, the face you had before your Grandmother was born?"

Ponder this question now for a moment. How does it influence your breathing? And when you find yourself becoming tense and anxious, instead of trying to change the situation, simply welcome it as a reminder to return to the koan, the question, again as you look within. What was your original face? Who were you before your body appeared? Who are you now?

Living with the Questions

One does not have to be a mystic to explore questions such as those at the end of the last chapter. Whatever religious or spiritual beliefs we may have, in actuality we know nothing about *who* or *what we really are*, how we got here, why we're here, and what our destiny is. The fact that we *are* and anything *is* at all goes well beyond our comprehension. And that is fortunate. For if we can begin to pay attention to these questions resonating deep within us at the same moment we pay attention to the so-called outer world and do whatever is necessary in our lives, the miraculous— a sense of joyful, infinite potential—can be felt at a very deep level. Try it again now. Without expecting any mental answer, ask yourself: What was my original face? Who am I?

Can you begin to live with these questions—questions that call you toward the unknown in yourself? Can you feel them in the course of your everyday life? Of course you can! All it takes is inner sincerity and the realization that you don't really know yourself. It can be helpful to set yourself daily reminders. For example, make a pact with yourself to try it every hour on the hour between 9 a.m. and 4 p.m. The main thing is to practice on a daily basis.

Returning to the Unknown in Ourselves

Returning to the unknown in ourselves needs practice, for we have little experience of it and there is little in the structure of society that supports it. A big support in this return is your breath. You can start with noticing the movements of your breath and following your in-breath as it disappears into the expanding energy field and space of your body, especially your belly and heart. To help with this process, put one hand on your belly and the other on your heart. Then, as you follow your out-breath, simply observe and let go of all the ideas and attitudes you have about yourself and others at that moment and *come to rest for a moment in not knowing*. Let yourself come to a kind of *inner stop*. Then simply allow the in-breath to arise on its own, when it is ready.

Try this now for several breaths as you turn your attention inward toward the dimension of yourself that can welcome without commentary whatever is happening at the moment, whether it is in your estimation positive, negative, or neutral. Try it during the day, too. You can include it in the "Living with the Questions" practice we just discussed.

Looking toward the No-Thing that You Are

The awareness of the "breath of life" as it moves through us draws us immediately (if we pay attention) toward something far greater than the paltry little mental, emotional, or physical "I" that we habitually call ourselves. By spending several minutes each day directing your attention inward toward the underlying energies of the "breath of life"—including the physical movements of inhalation, exhalation, and the brief but natural resting place before the next inhalation—you will become quieter inside and more present to yourself as you are. This will enable you to look even deeper inside toward the "no-thing" that you are in your very essence. It will enable you to look toward what you experience when you are *zero distance* from yourself, toward the silent, spacious receptivity, the pure, impartial awareness, that lies at the heart of being— the simple, undefined, unqualified, I AM. Can you experience this right now as you follow your exhalations and inhalations for at least five minutes?

Noticing that You Often Hold Your Breath

As you practice following your breath now (and in the many other circumstances of your life), you will no doubt notice that you sometimes hold your breath when you shift from one emotion to another, or when you move from one location or event to another, or when you feel a moment of anxiety or uncertainty as you switch from one activity or goal to another. Given that our lives are filled with many such transitions, and given that we live in a social and political climate of chronic anxiety and stress, the end result is that, when we look, we often find ourselves holding our breath. So check in on your breathing now. Are you holding your breath? In general, breath holding eventually constricts and weakens the breathing muscles and undermines their coordination. Check in frequently during your waking hours.

Frequent Breath Holding Reveals a Fundamental Disharmony

Frequent breath holding is not only unhealthy (and often leads in the very next moment to excessively fast, upper-chest breathing) but it also reveals a fundamental disharmony in the way we experience ourselves and the world. Holding our breath is often the nervous system's way of helping us listen for potential danger, of putting us on high alert for something that may threaten us.

Take a moment now to imagine yourself alone in your bed late at night. Suddenly you hear an unexpected sound some-place in your home. What happens inside your mind and body? The first thing you will probably do is hold your breath so that you can better hear whether danger is present. You will probably also sense tension throughout your muscles—as though you are preparing to take some kind of action. In today's world, filled as it is with instant communication from around the world about all the perils we face, many of us, for the most part unconsciously, now listen for danger night and day, and so we hold our breath a lot and are filled with tension. We need to see this mechanism in action *in ourselves*.

So, next time you catch yourself holding your breath, before reacting by breathing again take an inner snapshot of your entire body and mind. Notice what tensions, emotions, and thoughts are acting on you. This can all be done in an instant— through presence. Being present to what is actually happening inside you will help free you from these tensions, emotions, and thoughts, and you will effortlessly find yourself breathing in a natural, spontaneous way again.

Following Your Breath through the Transitions in Your Life

Living now is never a static experience, since the spaciousness of now is always filled with new contents. An important practice you can try on a regular basis is simply to notice what happens to your breathing as you shift from one activity or goal to another during your day. You can start by noticing whether you hold your breath as you arise from your chair, bed, or couch. You can also notice your breath when you move from one bit of news to another in the newspaper or while watching TV. At the same time, notice any anxiety, apprehension, tension and so on that may be occurring.

Try it right now. After reading this sentence, and while staying in touch with your breathing, get up from your chair or wherever you are reading and make that call or write that letter you have been putting off because of some kind of unpleasantness associated with it.

There are very few times when it's really necessary to hold your breath (hearing an unexplained sound in our house late at night may well be one of them). The simple noticing of your breath as you change your position, begin a new movement, or alter your mental focus will itself help ensure that you keep breathing through the many transitions in your day. What's more, this noticing will activate the inner space of presence, a spacious awareness that helps you remain awake simultaneously to yourself and the world.

Your Body Has Many Breathing Spaces

Your breath is a direct path to the sense of inner spacious awareness. As you begin to pay more attention to it, you will notice that your body itself is a huge breathing space, made up of smaller spaces such as your chest, back, belly, and pelvis. Though we were designed to breathe utilizing all of these spaces to varying degrees, the movement of the breath likes to go where there is ease and comfort. When one or another area is tight or uncomfortable, which is often associated with negative or anxious thoughts and emotions, as well as with any past physical or emotional traumas, the movement of the breath has a difficult time engaging that area, and so our breath becomes unbalanced or disharmonious in some way.

See if you can notice now any areas in your body where your breathing seems impeded or restricted. Pay particular attention to your belly and back. And, whenever you can remember to do so at other times of the day, notice whether certain thoughts, emotions, postures, movements, situations, conversations, news, and so on have the effect of opening or constricting your overall sense of your breathing spaces.

It may be helpful to keep a breathing diary. Write down how you experience your breathing spaces in different situations and with different people. Over time you will discover that awareness of the changing nature of your breath helps awaken a more intimate relationship with all the aspects of your life.

Observing the Tension in Your Eyes, Face, and Throat

As we follow our breath more often through our daily activities, we will discover that we live in our thoughts and reactive emotions much of the time—the associative internal judgments, commentaries, and stories that occupy so much of our lives. Concomitantly, we will discover that our center of gravity is usually up in our heads, eyes, faces, throats, and upper chest. As a result, many of us carry an enormous amount of unconscious tension in these areas, and this tension influences not only our breathing but also the flow of energy throughout our body. What's more, living in our thoughts and reactive emotions buffers us from true, living impressions of ourselves and others.

Sense your eyes right now. How do they feel? Are they tense? Are they relaxed? Take a minute or two to find out. When you are clear about how your eyes feel, sense your throat. How does it feel? Does it feel constricted in any way? When we are tense or constricted anywhere in our eyes or throat, our jaw is often also tense. So sense the area of your jaw on both sides of your face right now. How does your jaw feel? Does it feel loose and relaxed or tight and tense? Now, staying in touch with your eyes, jaw, and throat at the same time, check your breathing. How does it feel? Are there any constrictions in your breathing? Don't attempt to change anything; simply be present to what is actually occurring.

Becoming More Aware of Your Eyes

Now let's go a bit deeper. Your eyes play a huge role in how the breath of life moves through you. Not only does much of what you experience of the world come directly through your eyes, often called the "doorway to the soul," but they are linked directly to your autonomic nervous system, the part of your nervous system that regulates much of the functioning of your organs and glands. When your eyes are tense, the signals they send to your nervous system help prepare you for some kind of evasive or protective action. This of course puts you in a hypervigilant state of readiness to flee or fight or freeze. At such moments, many people hold their breath or begin to breathe faster.

Close your eyes for a moment and sense what they feel like. Are they relaxed and comfortable, or tense and uncomfortable?

Just notice. Now open them and sense them again. How do they feel? Check in on your breathing. How does it feel?

Relaxing Your Eyes

Now you're going to learn some simple techniques for relaxing your eyes, which will have a powerful impact not only on your breathing but also on your very awareness.

If you are wearing glasses, please take them off. Close your eyes and gently and slowly rotate or spiral them in as many different directions as you can. Check your breathing as you do so. Then, with your eyes still closed, make a figure eight with the movement of your eyes, again checking your breathing. First make several figure eights on the horizontal plane; then make several on the vertical plane. Finally, rub your hands together until they are very warm and energized and place your right palm gently over your right eye and your left palm gently over your left eye. The fingers of each hand will be on your forehead, and the base of each hand will be on the corresponding cheekbone. The center of each palm should be over the eye, but not actually touching it. Feel the warmth coming from your hands into your eyes, and simply allow your eyes to relax back fully into their sockets. Now repeat the entire procedure with your eyes opened. Then repeat it again with them closed. When your eyes feel totally relaxed, check your breathing again. How does it feel now? Are you breathing any differently than you were before you undertook this practice?

Becoming More Aware of Your Jaw and Throat

Now that your eyes are more relaxed, notice how your jaw feels (it may already be a bit more relaxed than it was earlier). In particular, see if you can sense the temporal mandibular joint (TMJ) of your jaw, that enormously complex joint—said to have fifty-six moving parts—on both sides of your face below your ears. Voice scientists have pointed out that this joint can generate from six thousand to ten thousand pounds of force per square inch. If you grind your teeth at night, it is this joint that is involved. A tense jaw not only signals some kind of mental or emotional disturbance, but it also helps maintain it.

Now check your throat, especially the area right around your Adam's apple down to the top of your sternum. Take a minute or so to sense how this area feels. The throat area includes the thyroid and parathyroid glands that, among other things, help regulate our metabolic functions. A chronically tense throat not only constricts our breath, but also throws our metabolism out of whack. A tense throat can signal an identification with or attachment to fear or anxiety concerning communication. Our throat often gets tense not just when we are communicating or thinking about communicating with others, especially those with whom we are experiencing some kind of discord, but also when we carry on any kind of troubled internal dialogue with ourselves.

Relaxing Your Jaw and Throat

Now that you have a general sensation of your jaw and throat, tense your jaw intentionally for at least thirty seconds and simultaneously check your breathing. Take several breaths as you maintain a tense jaw and notice how the tension influences your breathing. Now let your jaw relax for several more breaths.

To support this relaxation process, open and close your mouth several times and then let your chin drop downward naturally and your mouth remain open. Take several breaths through your nose and mouth in this position. Then bring your chin back up to its normal position and experiment with your fingers touching and massaging the mandibular joint as you slowly and repeatedly open and close your mouth for at least thirty seconds. Then rotate and move your jaw in as many ways and directions as you can for another thirty seconds. Then stop any work with your jaw. How does your jaw feel now? What about your breathing?

Now stick out your tongue as far as you can several times. Move it around in as many directions as possible. Then let it relax into the bottom of your mouth. Use your hands to massage a bit around your throat. Make several gentle but audible yawning sounds, starting with a relatively high pitch and gradually lowering it as the sound develops. Ahhhhhhhhh. Ahhhhhhhhh. Ahhhhhhhhh. How do your mouth, jaw, and throat feel now?

Take several breaths through your relaxed mouth and throat and see how your breathing feels. Then close your mouth gently, allowing your jaw, mouth, and throat to remain relaxed. Again check your breathing as you now breathe gently and quietly through your nose. This experiment shows quite clearly how your breathing is influenced by any tensions in your mouth, jaw, and throat.

If you want to breathe in a freer, more natural way, so that the breath of life can move through you fully, you will need to find ways to release the many unnecessary tensions not just in your eyes, jaw, tongue, and throat, but also throughout your body. For these tensions constrict your breathing, distract your brain and nervous system, consume your energy, and make it more difficult to be who you really are in your essence. If you try this practice for a couple of minutes each day, not only will you help keep the upper breathing space more relaxed, which will help your breathing, but you will also strengthen your inner attention and awareness.

Awakening Your Center of Gravity in the Breathing Space of the Belly

Though all the breathing spaces of the body must be free to engage with each breath, the foundation of our breath lies in the lower space physically located just below the navel, in the area of what is called the Hara (in Chinese, the Lower Tan Tien), one of the main energy centers of the body. From a physiological standpoint, this area is also our center of gravity.

To begin awakening this area, rub your hands together until they are very warm. Then place one hand over the other touching your navel area. Sense the warmth and energy coming from your hands, and let the warmth and energy spread through your entire abdomen and back into your spine. Notice how the warmth in the abdominal area makes you more naturally comfortable and influences your breathing. What happens as you inhale? What happens as you exhale? Just be present to this process for several breaths without attempting to change anything.

Allowing Your Belly to Expand and Retract on Inhalation and Exhalation

Breath is not just movement of air and tissue, it is also movement of the life force. As your belly becomes warmer and more relaxed, you may notice that it expands more as you inhale and retracts more as you exhale. Let these movements take place by themselves. As we will explore further later, the natural expansion and retraction of the belly on inhalation and exhalation helps the diaphragm move more completely through its entire range of motion.

Rub your hands again until they are warm, place them on your navel, and notice what happens on inhalation and exhalation. Whatever you do, however, do not use any kind of force or willfulness to try to move your belly. Just let the touch, warmth, and energy from your hands help attract the movement of your breath into the belly area. Allow your attention to go deep inside your belly to see what the opening and closing of this area on inhalation and exhalation feels like. Notice how the opening and closing takes place not only from front to back but also from side to side. Continue in this way for at least five minutes, and notice how your breathing naturally slows down and becomes fuller. Notice also how this simple, natural action helps to lower your center of gravity and connect you with the earth.

Finding Your True Center of Gravity with the Earth's Help

For our center of gravity to begin to drop from the head, throat, and upper chest to the belly area, the Hara, we need not only to learn how to sense our bellies more often, but we also need to begin *to feel ourselves* (at least at one level) as part of all organic life on earth, the vast interrelated system of nature's complex metabolism. As part of this system, we need to learn how to let the earth support us and energize us consciously as we move through the various transitions of our lives. This requires *coming home to ourselves*. It requires discovering inner security and stability in presence itself, which is only possible *now*, at this very moment. This coming home to our own presence represents a major transformation in how we experience ourselves, since, for the most part, we believe that it is only through constant doing to achieve some future goal that we can find true meaning and happiness.

The fact is, of course, that at the physical, bodily level we are supported at every moment by the earth and its powerful vibratory field. Lost as we are, however, in the many judgmental thoughts, emotions, and stories that consume our attention, we live as though we were not so supported. In fact, much of the time, except during moments of pain or pleasure, we live as though we don't even have bodies. And this produces a great deal of unnecessary tension in our lives—tension that restricts our breathing, our energy, and our consciousness.

So take a few minutes now to ponder your situation. Realize that you are supported by the earth and that this support is unconditional—there is nothing you have to do. All that is required is recognizing what is already obvious—the *being-ness* of your experience. Realize also that your body is made from the same substances as those of the earth and its atmosphere, and that everything you have or are at the physical level is somehow dependent on an exchange with the earth and the life it sustains. As a breathing being, you are part of organic life on earth interconnected with everything that exists.

Sensing Your Weight Being Supported by the Earth

Next time you catch yourself thinking, feeling, moving, or breathing in an anxious and tense way, take a good look at this state without trying to figure out what caused it. Then let your shoulders relax and drop (they will invariably be a bit tense and up) and sense your feet on the ground or your butt on the chair or floor. Sense how your entire weight is being supported by the earth as your breathing takes place by itself. You can try it right now. What does it feel like? What sensations are there in your feet or buttocks and elsewhere in your body? What feelings take place as you become consciously aware of the earth supporting you as you breathe?

If you can stay with this experiment for several breaths, simply appreciating your connection with the earth, your self-image, which is generally based on a sense of separation from others and from the so-called objects that your senses reveal, will let go of its grip on you, and your breath will by itself expand lower into your abdomen and throughout your body.

Try this exercise as often as you can, and you will soon see many beneficial changes both in your breathing and in your relationship with yourself and others. You will also see that these changes are not produced by any kind of "doing" but by presence—the living perception of *what is*, without any stories about it.

Tension in Your Pelvic Floor Muscles Impedes Your Connection to the Earth

One of the obstacles to allowing the earth to support us fully is the unnecessary tension we carry unconsciously in the pelvic floor muscles. Of course, these tensions are inextricably tied in with our self-image, with the way we think and feel about ourselves and the world, and will release when we cease being so identified with it.

The muscles of the pelvic floor have many natural functions. They support the bladder, rectum, and some of the abdominal and sexual organs. Thus they are involved in everything from giving birth to expelling (or keeping from expelling) feces and urine, to lifting heavy objects, and to sexual activities and orgasm. But these muscles are also highly sensitive to the thoughts and emotions with which we habitually identify.

See if you can sense your pelvic floor muscles now. Let your awareness go deep inside your pelvic area and sense what is happening there. Do the muscles feel tight? Do they feel relaxed? Do you feel as though you are holding on to something with these muscles? At the same time, notice what is going on in your thoughts and emotions. Give yourself two or three minutes to explore your pelvis through simple awareness.

Constrictions in Your Pelvic Floor Muscles Impede Your Breathing

Since the pelvis is part of the lower breathing space, the pelvic floor muscles are also intimately involved in breathing. These muscles include the perineum, located between the anus and sexual organs, and the pelvic diaphragm, which stretches across the floor of the pelvic cavity. In healthy, natural breathing, during inhalation the diaphragm in the chest moves downward, the belly expands outward, the abdomen widens in all directions, and the pelvic floor moves slightly downward. During exhalation, the entire process is reversed, with the pelvic diaphragm moving slightly upward. If the pelvic floor is chronically tense or constricted in any way, a spontaneous, natural breath is not possible. The free movement through us of the breath of life requires a pelvic floor that is both relaxed and resilient.

What's more, the perineum is the site of the first chakra. An overly tight and contracted perineum often signals a sense of insecurity or loneliness. When it is dynamically relaxed and open, you will feel more grounded and rooted to the earth. You will also feel more of a sense of peacefulness. Many of our emotions are reflected in the perineum. With these ideas in mind, check your pelvic muscles again through simple awareness. Give yourself two or three minutes to notice what happens there as you breathe.

Squatting to Become More Aware of Your Pelvic Muscles

Many of us, of course, have little awareness of our pelvic floor muscles and thus are unaware of the chronic tension in them. For those who are in this situation, there are several approaches to gaining more awareness of these muscles, releasing unnecessary tension, and revitalizing them. A good practice you can begin immediately is to squat more often. You can do so while reading, watching TV, or having conversations with friends and family. When you squat, be sure to sense how your breathing engages the muscles in your pelvic floor.

Unless you have an injury that makes it impossible, try squatting now. If you cannot squat with both feet entirely on the ground, then squat using mainly the balls of your feet. If even this is difficult in a more or less upright position, then get in a kind of semi-squat position with a firm cushion under your heels or your hands on the floor in front of you to help support your weight and keep you balanced. Over time, as your feet, ankles, legs, pelvis, hips, and back begin to relax and perhaps become stronger, you will find yourself able to squat for longer periods with both feet flat on the ground. However you squat, notice how it helps to energize and bring you into relationship with the center of gravity in your belly. Pay special attention to where your breathing takes place as you squat. Notice the movements in your belly, back, pelvis, and chest on both the in-breath and the out-breath.

Working with Your Perineum to Open up Your Breathing

Another good practice you can experiment with is to sense your perineum area and quickly (a couple of times a second) tense and relax it. (Remember, this is the area between your anus and your sexual organs). You can do this wherever you are—sitting, standing, or lying down—but be sure that you allow the sensation of being supported by the earth to enter your awareness as you do so. Before beginning, however, check your breathing. Notice what it feels like. Then use your index finger to push gently but firmly into your perineum. Keeping your finger there, try contracting and relaxing the area. You should be able to feel some movement. If you have difficulty, just imagine that you have to use the toilet very badly and tense the muscles needed in order to keep this from happening. Then relax these muscles. Though this will activate many of your pelvic muscles, it will also help give you the sensation of your perineum. Contract and relax these muscles for a minute or so. Now check your breathing again. Perhaps it feels a bit fuller and more open. Do you feel more connected with the earth? If not, try again, more gently, with less effort.

Breathing from Your Pelvic Floor

Now that you can sense your pelvic floor area more fully, check your breathing again and notice any changes that have occurred. You will probably feel your in-breath originating from lower down in your abdomen. When the pelvic floor begins to relax and participate more in the breathing process, your breathing invariably becomes more natural and spontaneous.

To facilitate or deepen this experience, direct your attention inwardly to the area between your anus and your genitals (without the help of your finger) and have the sense that your inhalation begins there. No force or effort should be used in this practice. It is simply a matter of sensation, visualization, focus, and intention. Simply allow the inhalation to take place as though you were breathing from that area.

As you practice doing so, notice how your breath slows down a bit by itself and seems to fill more of your lower belly, back, and ribs. Just follow your breathing for three or four minutes as you keep your attention in the area of the perineum. Notice how this impacts your breathing and your sense of yourself. As the habitual tensions in this area begin to release more over time, and as your breathing begins to originate more consistently from lower down in your body, you will notice how this practice helps lower your center of gravity, making it more possible to be exactly where you are, instead of compulsively looking toward the future for some kind of change.

Living in Front of Ourselves

As I mentioned earlier, we often live in front of ourselves, with our attention directed toward the future. When our attention is primarily occupied with rejecting the present moment and changing something in the future, we are not much available for immediate contact with the vast, conscious embrace of space and silence that is who we really are at the deepest level. Such contact can only occur when we are able to accept the present moment as it is, when we are able to realize that *now* is the only time we will ever have.

Living in front of ourselves generally occurs when we become identified with (lost in) some thought, emotion, judgment, belief, or story about how things should be different than they are, about "what should be." If we observe ourselves at such moments, we will notice that the center of gravity of our breathing is primarily in the upper chest, which upsets the flow of life and energy throughout the body. What's more, we will notice that our breathing speeds up.

As an experiment, check in on your breathing. For several breaths just notice how your breath feels. Now think seriously of something that you've been putting off and really have to get done very soon in the future. Let yourself dwell on the importance of this project, and what you believe others will think or say or what will happen if it doesn't get done on time. Think about the obstacles to this project and about how you will accomplish it. Let yourself experience your usual tense or anxious state when such situations arise. Now check in on your breathing. How has it changed? How do you feel?

Now try a different experiment. Letting go of these thoughts, return to yourself exactly where you are. Put your hands on your belly and feel your weight being supported by the earth. Allow the sensation of your body, in whatever posture you are in, to enter your awareness. Take a few minutes to enjoy the sensation of just being where you are in that posture. Notice how your breath slows down and moves lower down in your body. Now, staying in touch with the sensation of just being where you are, think again about what needs to be done and notice how much quieter and intelligent these thoughts are. Notice how what others may think is not so important. The fact is, presence is transformational. It allows all of our functions—thinking, feeling, sensing—to operate more harmoniously.

Sensing Your Spine

Living in front of ourselves as we often do, we experience ourselves as disembodied and rather one dimensional, as though we were the flat (and reversed) image we see in a mirror. When we turn our attention backward, however, one of the first things we notice is that our body has a spine. We also notice that there is a rich field of sensory impressions located between the front of the face, throat, chest, and belly and the spine and the back of the head. Suddenly, we are *three* dimensional; we experience our own sensory depth.

Try it now. Simply sense your spine in a sitting or standing position. Notice areas where there is more or less sensation. Notice whether your breathing engages your spine. Does your spine move as you breathe? If so, what happens on inhalation? On exhalation?

Now sense your spine as you bend over slowly and gently from the waist. Let your head hang freely from your spine. Let your arms hang as well. As you experience your spine in this position, pay attention to your breathing. Where do you feel your breath? Does your breath engage your spine now? In what way? Breathe in this bent but relaxed position for several breaths. Then, when you feel you're ready, sit or stand in a vertical position and notice the new overall sensation of yourself that has appeared. In what ways do you feel different?

Hug Yourself

Accustomed as we are to living in front of ourselves, many of us have difficulty allowing our backs to breathe fully. After years of unawareness, we simply don't have the experience of what this feels like. There is a simple practice you can try now, however, that will help.

First, check in on your breathing. For several breaths just notice whether your back is involved. Now you're going to hug yourself. Place your right forearm under your left armpit and, if possible, grab your left shoulder blade with the fingers of your right hand. In this position your arm should be against your chest. Now reach across with your left arm and, if possible, grab your right shoulder blade with the fingers of your left hand. If you cannot reach around all the way to your shoulder blades, that's fine; just reach as far as possible. This will help compress your chest and stimulate you to breathe using other parts of your body.

While hugging yourself in this way, and for several breaths, notice which parts of your body are engaged in your breathing. You may notice, for instance, that you are breathing more in both your back and your belly. Just enjoy the sensations of these movements of your breath, especially in your back. Sense how your shoulder blades separate (widen) on the in-breath and return closer together on the out-breath. Sense how your spine moves back and seems to lengthen on the in-breath and returns on the out-breath. Notice how you begin to feel a sense of spaciousness in your back as you breathe.

Now let your arms drop down comfortably to your sides and again check in on your breathing. You will see that your back is now considerably more involved, opening as you inhale and closing as you exhale. Just enjoy these sensations of the breath of life moving through your body. You can try this simple practice as often as you like throughout the day, but especially when you seem to be living in front of yourself and feel anxious about the future.

Organic Relaxation

When I speak about enjoying the sensations of the breath of life moving through your body, what I am talking about, at least at one level, is the process of organic relaxation, of loosening the energetic knots that restrict our life force and keep our awareness bound to our thoughts and reactive emotions. It is through the deep enjoyment of organic relaxation that these knots begin to unravel and that what is superfluous in our lives—the unnecessary structures of thought, emotion, and sensation that we have constructed and identified with to support or defend our self-image—let go of their hold on us. Maintaining these structures by believing in what they tell us not only consumes our energy but also keeps us from *letting go into who we really are.*

To experience a sense of this relaxation, lie down comfortably on a mat or soft carpet with your hands on your belly. Check in on your breathing. As you do so, notice how you are completely supported by the earth. Really let yourself feel this support. Notice the thoughts and emotions that appear, along with the sensations of relaxation that are settling in. Just let them be as they are, without commenting on them or dwelling on them in any way.

Now pay particular attention to your back and spine. Take a few breaths to sense the interface, the vibratory sensation, between your back and the floor. Let your entire back release into the floor. Let your belly rise and fall with each inhalation and exhalation. Notice how your entire body, freed a bit from your identification with your thoughts, emotions, and efforts, begins to relax into emptiness and spaciousness. As this happens, you will sense your breath slowing down and becoming quieter, allowing a new, fuller sense of receptivity and presence to radiate from every aspect of your being. Notice also how more parts of your body are now involved effortlessly in your breath—and how you can now feel the multileveled movements of your breath inside the conscious spaciousness that you begin to sense is what you really are.

Awakening the Spine

Now, in this more relaxed posture, continue sensing your hands on your belly as it rises and falls. At the same time, sense how your lower spine in the area opposite your hands releases into the floor on the in-breath. Then allow it to relax even more into the floor as the out-breath takes place. Continue this process for the next several breaths.

Now move your hands up to your solar plexus, just beneath the breast bone (sternum), and, again, allow the spine to release downward on the in-breath, and relax even more into the floor on the out-breath. After several breaths, next move your hands to your lower chest, then to your middle chest, and finally to your upper chest, taking several breaths in each position and allowing the corresponding segments of the spine to release into the floor on inhalation and relax even more into the floor on exhalation.

Then, put your arms on the floor at your sides and experience yourself lying there, fully supported by the earth, as your breathing takes place in its own rhythm by itself. Sense all the movements taking place in your body, and especially in your spine. Does your spine feel longer, more alive? What has happened to your breathing? Do you feel more present, more accepting and available to yourself as you are?

Stretching, Breathing, and Opening from Your Core

Lie down comfortably on your back on a mat or soft carpet. Just relax into the earth's support. Once you feel completely present to yourself lying there, breathing, gently put your arms as straight behind you as possible on the floor pointing away from your head with your palms facing up. (If there is pain or excessive tension in your arms or shoulders as you do so, simply place your arms as far as back on the floor as you can without discomfort.) As you breathe in this posture, pay particular attention to the area around your navel, also called your "core."

When you are as comfortable as possible in this posture, and able to sense your breath moving through your core to some extent, undertake the following movements: As you inhale, stretch your right arm farther away from your head; as you exhale, let go of the stretch and simply let your arm relax. Then do the same with your right leg, left leg, and left arm in turn. Then do another round of stretching, but this time begin with the right leg and finish with the right arm. Then do a third round beginning with the left leg and finish with the right leg.

Then do a final round beginning with the left arm and finishing with the left leg. Then repeat the entire process at least two more times.

As you work in this way, your attention will be called to be more present to what is happening and less likely to be absorbed by your associative thoughts, images, and dreams. If it is too complicated at first to start each series with a different limb, then simply repeat the limbs several times in the same order until you are relaxed enough and your attention is free enough to undertake these movements in the order I have given.

After repeating this sequence several times, put your hands on your belly and check in on your breathing. How do you feel now? What is your breathing like? Do you feel closer, more present, to your entire body?

The "Vitruvian Man" Position

Still lying down, put your arms once again on the floor pointing away from your head. Take several breaths in this position. Now, simply as an experiment, spread your arms and legs at approximately a 45-degree angle, as in the famous drawing by Leonardo da Vinci, called "Vitruvian Man." Rest in this position for at least two minutes while staying in touch with your breathing.

Now, retaining the angle, stretch your right arm during inhalation and release it during exhalation. Then stretch your left leg during inhalation and release it during exhalation. Now do the same with your left arm and right leg. Take your time. Notice how these stretches move your body on the floor, almost as though you were a baby lying on its back just exploring and learning how to move and thoroughly enjoying the exploration.

Now stretch your right arm and left leg together on inhalation and release them on exhalation. Do the same with the left arm and right leg. Try this several times. Pay special attention to your core as you work in this way. Then return to stretching your arms and legs separately. Notice how the flow of breath through your body is influenced by these stretches. After about five or ten minutes, let your arms and legs rest where they are and simply be present to yourself as a whole being. What is happening now with the breath, body, thoughts, and feelings that you thought you knew so well? Perhaps you are experiencing (and enjoying) them in a new, more innocent and spacious way. Allow yourself to relax consciously into the immediacy of this spaciousness, becoming one with it.

The Smile of Compassion

As we relax consciously more and more into the immediacy of spaciousness, we may suddenly find all our so-called knowledge being replaced by a new, more honest sense of *not knowing*. It is not that our knowledge disappears or is seen to be worthless (obviously, it is quite valuable at its own level); no, it is that it is seen in a totally new light—the light of the vastness and ultimate unknowability of Truth. The belief that the mind could somehow understand itself, the universe, and God gives way to a spontaneous smile arising from deep within—a smile of compassion. It is as though consciousness itself smiles at us. Suddenly we realize what has always been true: we can never truly *know* ourselves as we know the objects around us, but we can *be* ourselves. And the conscious immediacy of this "be-ing" needs no knowledge—no thing—to validate it. To the contrary, this conscious immediacy of being is the meaning and truth for which we have always been searching. And at this moment, we know it at a very deep level. As we recognize this truth and smile at its utter simplicity, something opens in our heart—compassion not only for ourselves but for everyone who has ever lived or will live on this planet and who has shared or will share the breath of life with us.

Smile, Stretch, and Breathe

Of course, many of us have had moments of awakening. What is crucial, however, is learning how to allow and integrate such moments into our everyday life, including those moments when we find ourselves lost in negativity and unable to open to ourselves. Many of the practices in this book are oriented toward creating conditions that will make this integration more possible—and almost all of them rely on discovering a new relationship to that amazing temple of awareness we call the body and to the sensations through which we experience it.

Here is a simple integration practice you can undertake at your desk, standing, or lying down, and no matter what kind of mood you are in. To begin, check in on your breathing. Follow your breathing for a couple of minutes, sensing the spaciousness that opens with each in-breath and the emptying that takes place with each out-breath. Notice how, as you pay attention to these movements of your breath, your thoughts and emotions are somehow contained inside that sense of spaciousness and then released with the exhalation. You may suddenly find yourself experiencing a deep sense of appreciation for just being alive now and here. And this experience may well bring a smile to your face. If not, simply *put* a smile on your face (whether you feel like smiling or not) and start stretching. Stretch slowly and comfortably in as many ways as you can, using your intention and attention to direct your breath through your smile into whatever areas you are stretching. Do not hold your breath at any point during this practice! Just let your breathing be shaped and energized by the smile and the movements of your stretching. Be sure to stretch evenly in all directions—up, down, to the sides, and so on (depending, of course, on your position). And be sure to sense everything that is happening.

After a couple of minutes of stretching, and still smiling, see if you can slowly and gently stretch in new ways—perhaps from your liver, your heart, your kidneys, your tail bone, or your eyeballs (use your creativity to find new ways to stretch). Take your time. Work like this for at least five more minutes.

Now check in on your breathing again. Notice how your breath has become so even and quiet that it seems to draw you into the silence of not knowing, where any negativity toward yourself or others releases its grip on you and you suddenly realize that you have come home to the fundamental presence that you are.

Negativity: A Rejection of What Is

From the point of view of the spaciousness that lies at the heart of presence, negativity is simply a constriction or contraction. It is generally brought on by a rejection of "what is" by the mind, or by a deep-rooted identification with some judgment about what is being experienced. Each time you catch yourself about to be caught up in a negative judgment, thought, or emotion toward yourself or anyone else, simply sense yourself inhaling through your heart and exhaling (slowly and gently through pursed lips) appreciation, love, and compassion from the whole of yourself out into the world. Let your inhalation take place effortlessly through your nose, receiving and appreciating the air and energy that comes to you without any kind of grasping or trying. If you are in conditions that allow it, it may be helpful to put one or both hands on your heart as you experiment with this practice. Work in this way for at least nine complete breaths at a time.

You can undertake this practice as many times as you wish each day. The key is to be fully aware through sensation of all the movements that are occurring in your body without judging them in any way. As this awareness deepens, you will experience the sensation of your breath, of the breath of life as it moves through you, not only as a powerful support for presence but as an integral dimension of being itself.

The Childhood Breath

Think back to when you were a child. Unless you had asthma or some other health problem, the power of the life force, your breath, manifested itself in just about everything you did. Do you remember the kinds of things you did then? In addition to jumping, running, twisting, turning, swimming, dancing, skipping, hopping, wrestling, and all the other physical activities that help keep the ribcage, back, and diaphragm flexible and loose, you probably also remember hollering, shouting, and singing a lot—at least until your parents and teachers told you to stop. Perhaps you were even told your voice was so terrible that you shouldn't even consider singing. This has happened with many of us, and the results have often been devastating, not just on the physical and emotional levels, but also to the very core of one's self-esteem.

What your parents probably did not realize is that all of these activities, including the constant use of your voice in many different ways, were spontaneous developmental manifestations of the life force, which awakened subtle physical and emotional perceptions moving through and animating you. The movements and sounds also helped keep your diaphragm flexible and strong.

Of course, under the influence of "education" and "socialization," you learned to control or stifle these manifestations and live more in the straightjacket of your mind, the world of thoughts, concepts, and judgments, which gradually separated you in an artificial and unhealthy way from the life and energy of your body. Unless you went ahead and sang anyway and participated in daily physical flexibility-oriented activities throughout high school or college—activities such as dance, swimming, martial arts, and so on—the daily demands on your diaphragm diminished, and, as a result, it ceased to function in an optimal way.

Now close your eyes and imagine that you are a child again. Think of a place and time when you really felt like you were able to be yourself—a tree, a lake, a playground, a hill, a particular street, wherever you felt most comfortable. Once you feel settled there, jump, skip, hop, twist, turn, run, sing, and shout for five minutes—all in your imagination. Really sense what that feels like. Notice how your breathing changes.

Now stop and go someplace where you enjoy being alone and try the same thing—but this time not in your imagination but in reality. In full awareness of what is happening in your body, emotions, and thoughts, and for at least five minutes, let the breath of life move through you as you jump, sing, and so on. Then check your overall sensation. How do you feel? Do you feel more connected with yourself and the environment? What about your breathing? Can you somehow sense the movement of the diaphragm in your chest with each breath?

The Diaphragm: the Spiritual Muscle

Though people talk often about the diaphragm—that large, domed-shape muscle that functions as the floor of the chest cavity and the ceiling of the abdominal cavity—they seldom have any real sensation of its many actions. Through its complex three-dimensional vertical, horizontal, and angular movements, the diaphragm not only helps the body take in the oxygen it needs, but it also helps the body rid itself of various waste products. Through these same movements, a healthy, well-developed diaphragm also helps to open and close the various breathing spaces of the body; release muscle tensions in the chest and back; support the nervous system, the cardiovascular system, the digestive system, and the immune system; and communicate verbally from deep within. A poorly functioning diaphragm makes it difficult for the breath of life to flow through us and express itself in a free and healthy way.

Except for our very first inhalation at birth, whenever the diaphragm is functioning well the in-breath happens as a spontaneous reflex that occurs after a full exhalation. Having emptied our lungs of everything that is no longer necessary, we are spontaneously and effortlessly filled again with fresh air. Perhaps that is one of the reasons some teachers call the diaphragm *a spiritual muscle* and use the analogy of the diaphragm to explain what happens when we learn to let go of the thoughts and emotions that keep us imprisoned in our self-image.

Follow your breath now for a few minutes, and pay special attention to what happens as you exhale. Do you feel that your exhalation is complete, or does it seem to stop prematurely? Do you try to grab for air willfully at the end of the exhalation or does the inhalation occur by itself in the form of a wave arising from the unknown? Just take note of what actually happens.

How the Diaphragm Works

The lungs sit on top of the diaphragm, a very powerful muscle that is fixed to the lower ribs, sternum, lumbar vertebrae, and so on. When we inhale, and if our diaphragm is in good health, it normally contracts, and the dome of the diaphragm flattens downward against the viscera (other movements take place as well, since the diaphragm always moves in three dimensions). It is this flattening that allows the lungs to expand to receive fresh air. Then when we exhale, and as a result of its elasticity and the viscera pushing against it, the diaphragm relaxes upward against the lungs, helping to expel old air from them. In other words, when we are breathing well the dome of the diaphragm first contracts downward during inhalation to allow the lungs to expand more fully, and then relaxes upward, pushing on the bottom of the lungs to help the lungs empty (except for the *residual volume* that is necessary to keep them from collapsing). The changing thoracic pressures, greatly influenced by the movements of the diaphragm, help regulate the movement of air in and out of our lungs and, of course, through our vocal cords as we speak, sing, and so on.

See if you can sense this process taking place as you follow your breath for the next five minutes. Does your breathing feel open and free or closed and constricted?

How Your Belly Impacts Your Diaphragm

If you have a tight belly, one that does not easily and freely expand outward as you inhale, the diaphragm will have a more difficult time moving downward because it is being resisted by the contracted abdominal muscles and the viscera. (Everything touches something else, and a movement or constriction in one place influences everything around it.) When you relax your belly and allow it to expand as you inhale, your viscera drop slightly down and out, and the diaphragm can more easily contract downward. Then, when exhalation takes place, the diaphragm begins its upward movement of relaxation, aided by the natural movement of the belly and viscera as they return toward the spine. This is called natural diaphragmatic or abdominal breathing. If your diaphragm is weak, however, or if your abdominal muscles are contracted or held very tightly, you will have less diaphragmatic contraction and movement downward during inhalation and thus less diaphragmatic elasticity and movement upward during exhalation.

As an experiment to see how your belly influences your breathing, suck in your belly now and try to inhale deeply (be careful not to do it too strenuously, as you can hurt yourself). How does this feel? Does it make breathing easier? Then relax your belly, put both hands on it, and allow it to expand as you inhale. Notice any differences. The fact is that, with your belly held very tightly, there will be much less downward movement of your diaphragm on inhalation since there is so much resistance from the abdominal muscles and viscera. And, if there is little downward movement on inhalation, there will be little upward movement on exhalation. So you will feel a lot of tension and effort in your breathing, which will often become less efficient, shallower, and faster, driven mainly by the secondary breathing muscles of the ribcage.

Unfortunately, as a result of more and more perceived mental and emotional stress in our lives and our frequent attempts to escape it by resisting what is actually happening—as well as of the common image of the flat, hard belly that is so prevalent today—people carry a lot of unnecessary tension in their bellies. Over time, this tension, combined with unnecessary tensions in the face, throat, chest, and back, constricts the diaphragm and makes it difficult for it to move in a balanced, harmonious way. A lot of this tension is created, of course, by the over-stimulation of our sympathetic nervous system—which kicks our "flight or fight or freeze" response into action. Eventually, this diminished movement of the diaphragm becomes the norm for many people, and the diaphragm in fact weakens and loses its ability to move through its entire potential range of motion (some five to six inches in the vertical direction), which means it often becomes incapable of moving fully downward or fully upward during the in-breath and out-breath. When the diaphragm is unable to move freely and easily through its entire potential range of vertical motion, both our inhalation and our exhalation suffer, and so does our voice. In time, our health and well-being suffer as well. It is important to point out that it is not just the vertical movements of the diaphragm that become restricted. The horizontal and angular movements, as well as the shape and size of the diaphragm, are also adversely affected.

Learning to Listen to the Functioning of the Diaphragm

As you become more present to yourself, it is possible to "listen" to the functioning of your own diaphragm and that of others while speaking, singing, chanting, and so on. For the quality and power of the sounds you make depend in large part on the quality and power of your breath.

An interesting experiment is to sense your breathing when you are very emotional. An effective way to do this is to listen to the quality and pitch of the words you speak and the sounds you make. Also, notice the tensions in your throat. We often tense our throat muscles to speak when our breathing has become inefficient or disharmonized and we have insufficient breath. We end up with excessive tension in our vocal cords as we try to express ourselves. Real self-expression is powered by our breath, not by our throat muscles and vocal chords.

As an experiment, recite out loud a poem you know well, or perhaps say the Lord's Prayer. Listen to how it sounds both internally and externally. Or, if you like, while you are alone say out loud what it is you would really like to say to someone but have been unable to do. Try it several times.

Now, either standing or sitting, sense your feet on the floor or your butt on the chair. Whatever position you are in, allow yourself to sense that you are being supported by the earth. Then, as you exhale fully, ask yourself the question—Who Am I?—that you asked earlier. Let yourself really feel this question; in other words, let it actually begin to live in you. Feel that you are in essence that which is conscious of and welcomes whatever appears. Then speak again more or less the same poem or words that you did above. Notice how your voice has changed and become more resonant, how it vibrates with the breath of presence. Try this several times.

Filling a Cup that Is Already Full

There is a well-known Taoist story that bears not only on how we breathe, but, just as importantly, on how we live. A student came to a venerable old Taoist master and asked if she would teach him. The master just looked at the student and asked him if he would like a cup of tea. When the student nodded yes, the master started pouring. As the student watched, however, he saw that even after the teacup was full the master kept pouring, and the tea was spreading all over the table and spilling to the ground. In the student's mind, he began to wonder if the master was simply not paying attention or if she was perhaps becoming senile. This may not be the master for me, he thought to himself. Finally, in exasperation he cried out, "Master, please, the cup is already full!" With compassionate eyes, the master simply looked at him and said, "Indeed, it most certainly is. How will you be capable of learning anything at all?"

Breathe into Being

All of us can laugh at this little story. Unfortunately, many of us may not immediately see how much it applies both to our breathing and to the way we live. A full inhalation cannot occur without a full exhalation. If our lungs are filled with old air, inhalation of fresh air cannot take place. So it is imperative to learn how to empty our lungs as fully and naturally as possible. Analogously, if our minds are filled with old beliefs, ideas, assumptions, and perceptions, it will be very difficult to take in anything new.

As we saw earlier, giving and receiving go hand in hand. If our giving is not full and complete—with no expectation of getting something as a result—what we receive will simply blend with whatever we have already received throughout our lives, and its substance, its essence, will either be diluted or never really experienced for what it actually is.

Ponder for a moment your breathing and your life. Do *you* really know how to let go of your last breath, your last thought, or your last emotion and receive your next breath, thought, or emotion in all of its freshness? Can you be present at this very moment to the miracle of what is happening, or is your presence somehow restricted by your identification with what you assume you already know? Try it now. Just follow your breathing for a few minutes and be honest about what you see.

Exhaling Consciously

The secret to healthy breathing is in learning how to exhale fully and effortlessly, so that the lungs are emptied except for the small residual volume needed to keep them from collapsing. In today's high-stress world, however, many of us never really exhale fully; we never really let go. In clinging to our self-image, and to the thoughts, emotions, fears, anxieties, and attitudes that support it, we often cling to static forms of breathing as well, not allowing the breath of life to move through us freely. This clinging signals a lack of spaciousness in us, an inability to let go into the unknown.

Check in on your breathing for a few breaths. What do your inhalations and exhalations feel like? Are they rhythmical, relaxed, and comfortable? Or are they jagged and tense? Just notice without attempting to change anything.

Now rub your hands together until they are very warm, and put them on your belly. Allow the warmth from your hands to spread throughout your abdomen. With full awareness of your hands on your belly, visualize a beautiful flower a few inches from your face, and gently blow through pursed lips just strongly enough to see the petals of the flower dance delicately with your breath. Continue to blow without tightening your belly until you have a comfortable amount of breath left, and then simply stop blowing as you sense your need for air and your next inhalation about to arise. After your inhalation arises spontaneously, gently blow on the flower again. Continue in this way for at least seven breaths. Then simply stop and observe how you feel. What is your breathing like now? What changes have occurred? Do you feel both a bit emptier and a bit more present?

The Emptiness of Presence

Paradoxically, real presence depends on exhaling, on emptying, on releasing our self-image so that we can be available to "what is." If we are *full of ourselves*, as the student was who visited the Taoist master in the story recounted earlier, we will be unable to see, hear, or feel anything that does not vibrate within the same frequency range as that of our self-image. Our self-image, the inner attitude (whether conscious or unconscious) that we have toward ourselves, habitually screens out anything that is not in harmony with it. It acts as a kind of *psychological buffer* to ensure that our ways of thinking, feeling, and perceiving are not put into question. It allows us always "to be right." Only a huge shock in our life or deep work with awareness will create a crack in our self-image so that we can see the truth and something new can enter.

When we work consciously with our breath, however, each inhalation gives us an opportunity to be drawn inward into the many physical and energetic dimensions of our bodies, and each exhalation gives us an opportunity to return home to our fundamental emptiness, to let go into the conscious underlying spaciousness and silence that is who we are at the deepest level. We see that we are really two-natured—form and emptiness—and that the two natures are somehow one. With this in mind, try the Exhaling Consciously practice again (see above chapter) in the simplest way you can. Take your time. There may come a point where you realize that the inhalation and exhalation are really one—a flowering of the presence that we are and have always been.

Common Obstacles to Working with Your Breath

As you work with some of the practices in this book, you may feel that your breathing seems too intentional and that you quickly get tired. You may experience, for example, that focusing on your breath in this way actually seems constricting. This is a common occurrence and can happen for several reasons.

One reason, of course, is that you may simply be trying too hard, and that instead of following your inhalations and exhalations as they move inside your awareness, you are actually attempting to manipulate them with your will. This kind of willful focusing actually diminishes the movement of your diaphragm, and it is one of the reasons I constantly emphasize the importance of listening and following, instead of doing.

Another reason may have to do with constrictions in the breathing spaces of the body, which we have referred to and worked with in earlier chapters. These constrictions are the result of our education and upbringing; they manifest themselves quite clearly in our postures, movements, voice, and other functions. Here it is not only imperative to see and free yourself from the various restrictive thoughts and emotions that comprise your self-image, but it may also be helpful to undertake tai chi, yoga, qigong, breathing therapy, hands-on body work, or some other kind of on-going work that can help you open up these spaces.

A third and very common reason you may feel constricted in doing the exercises is that your diaphragm may have become weakened over the years and may not be well coordinated with the other muscles involved in breathing. The practices in this book can help immensely with coordination of the breathing muscles. The work with special postures, movements, and sounds that I offer in these final chapters can also help.

Releasing Constrictions and Increasing Energy in the Upper Chest and Spine

As we have seen, for many of us our center of gravity is in our upper chest. This is also where many of us experience our so-called will and the frequent tension that goes with it. We often move into the future and through the world head or chest first, some of us even bent over at the waist, and are constantly on guard not to be toppled over by the natural shocks of life. Sometimes we even believe that if we can just try harder we can accomplish our goals. And it is true, we sometimes can. But this "trying harder" often generates enormous and unnecessary resistance, which often results in tensions in our upper chest, spine, throat, and face. And this tension impedes not only the harmonious functioning of the diaphragm but also the energy circulating through our bodies.

As an experiment, stand now with your feet about hip or shoulder width apart and put your arms straight out to your sides at a 90-degree angle to your body. Fix your eyes on a point in the distance as you keep your head centered on the midline of your body. Turn your right palm down toward the earth and your left palm up toward the heavens. Now simply hold this posture for as long as you can as you breathe gently through your nose. When it becomes too uncomfortable to continue, slowly raise your arms above your head until the back of your right hand touches the palm of your left hand. Take several breaths in this position, and then slowly lower your arms to your sides.

To finish, use either the palms of your hands or the inside of your fists to pound the various front and side parts of your chest as you tone the sound "Haaaaaaaa" so that it can be clearly heard across the room. You should be able to hear the effect of hitting your chest in the sound you are making. Stop pounding when you have about 10 percent of your air left, and finish exhaling though your nose as you return your arms to your sides. In this position, let your breathing normalize itself for three or four breaths as you breathe through your nose. Then repeat the pounding and the normalization of your breath two more times. When you are finished, check in on your breathing and notice the changes that have taken place, not just in your breathing but also in your overall sensation of yourself.

Though both of these practices (the arms out to the sides and the pounding of the chest) can be done separately (especially the pounding of the chest), together they offer a safe, powerful way to release the tensions in your upper chest and back and help the energy circulate throughout your body. Holding the arms out to the sides in the way described helps release the constrictions in the upper chest and spine, and pounding on your chest while toning the sound "Haaaaaaa" releases any residual tension from the exercise and also helps move energy through the energy channels that go through the chest. As you continue practicing on a daily basis you eventually want to reach the point where you are able to hold your arms out to the sides for at least fifteen minutes without discomfort.

Being Lifted by the Breath of Presence

Because many of us carry so much tension in our minds and bodies, holding your arms out to your sides for more than a couple of minutes may prove difficult if you try to do so using your muscles alone. What is necessary if you are to undertake this practice in an effortless way is an entirely new relationship to yourself—a relationship in which your arms are lifted by the breath of presence itself, not by your willpower.

What does this mean? First of all it means that you must be consciously present to yourself, just as you are in reality. For example, whether you are aware of it or not, you are always being supported by the earth. So let go of trying to hold yourself up. Notice and let go of the unnecessary mental and emotional baggage involved in this "holding." Simply observe how, as you relax, your own muscles keep you more or less upright in relation to the force of gravity. Let yourself experience that now. Feel your feet flat on the ground as you lift your arms straight out to your sides on the in-breath (right palm down, left palm up). Sense the two motions simultaneously—the release of your weight into the earth and the lifting of your arms to your sides during the inhalation. As you exhale, put even more attention on the release of your weight into the earth.

Now, continuing to breathe slowly and easily through your nose and with your arms remaining out to the sides, scan your body slowly from top to bottom with your awareness, letting any tension sink downward toward your feet and into the earth. Start with the very top of your head and move slowly down through your forehead, eyes, back of skull, jaw, neck, shoulders, arms and hands, chest, back, belly, pelvis, legs, and feet. Spend a bit more time with your shoulders, shoulder blades, and arms.

As you experience the ice-like sensation of a tension, let it melt from the heat of your awareness and release like water moving downhill through its natural course. Scan your entire body in this way. Notice how the more relaxed and present you are, the easier it is to hold up your arms.

At some point during this practice, you will feel, perhaps more than ever, a sense of "I AM," a sense that who you are at the deepest level is pure being, pure awareness, pure emptiness, pure silence. You may also sense that it is not your willpower holding up your arms, but the breath of presence itself. Stay in this posture for as long as is comfortable.

When you are ready to stop the practice, bring your arms up slowly over your head on the in-breath, letting the back of your right hand touch the palm of your left hand, and then slowly lower your arms to your sides on the out-breath. Remain standing for at least five more minutes, simply breathing and being who you already are.

We Are Two-Natured Beings

However we may view ourselves, and whether or not we believe in a personal or impersonal God, it is clear, as I pointed out earlier, that in some mysterious way we are two-natured beings—emptiness and form, space and substance, consciousness and the objects of consciousness, silence and sound, background and foreground, heaven and earth, and so on. As human beings, our ultimate possibility is to experience consciously the ever-present unity, or perhaps more accurately the *nonduality*, of these two natures in our everyday lives. For it is only then that we can truly be who we really are. Unfortunately, our society—and even our religions—often condition us to pay more attention to the objects in the foreground of our experience than to the vast depths of the unknown from which they manifest.

There are, of course, many ways to explore the truth of the nonduality of our two-natured being—meditation, prayer, self-inquiry, and so on. In this book we have been exploring this truth through the breath of being manifesting through the body at every moment. Before we finish this exploration, however, I would like to offer two more practices that will provide you with a profound way of experiencing the connection of heaven and earth, emptiness and form, in yourself. Before you move on, however, return to your body and check in on your breathing. Pay special attention to the way in which your breath arises from and returns to the unknown, from the spacious silence that you have begun to experience deep within.

The Conscious Body

Strangely enough, and perhaps counterintuitively, one of the most profound ways to experience our own emptiness is through the substance of body itself, especially the conscious body. Through becoming more intimate with the various sensations of your body, you will awaken to the silence, the spaciousness, that lies at its core. But for this to happen, you will need to release the inner tensions and contractions that maintain your habitual body image as a solid object somehow separate from your mind.

Stand now with your feet parallel about hip width apart and knees slightly bent. Sense your feet firmly on the ground, and rock backward and forward and side to side until your ankle joints feel soft and comfortable, as though resting on cushions or springs. Starting from the very top of your head, take at least ten minutes to scan your entire body with your conscious attention from head to foot. Do not hold your breath as you scan your body. Just allow your breathing to continue. When you find an area of tension or discomfort—an area that feels hard or ice-like—simply shine the warm light of your attention on that area until the ice-like sensation dissolves by itself and becomes fluid. Then simply sense the fluid sensation flowing downward like water to the next area of tension or discomfort, and repeat the entire process. Don't rush, and don't stop until you have released everything down beneath your feet and into the earth. Experience how your impressions of your body become emptier and emptier as your awareness dissolves any unnecessary tensions and contractions. As you relate to yourself in this way you will find your body and breath becoming more and more transparent and empty, and you will find yourself sensing that you are somehow "connecting heaven and earth." This will not merely be experienced as a thought, but, more importantly, as a direct sensation.

Connecting Heaven and Earth

The earth supports us at every moment of our lives, though most of the time we are completely ignorant of its support. And heaven—consciousness, spaciousness, emptiness—is the enlightened background and spiritual essence of our being. In this simple practice you will have an opportunity to experience in a nondual way both of these dimensions of yourself.

In the same standing position with which you just experimented, and looking straight ahead, raise your arms slowly up in front of you during your entire in-breath until they are directly overhead. At the very end of the in-breath, flatten your palms and push them upward as though you were holding up the heavens. On the out-breath, slowly bring your arms back down in front of you. Try this several times, waiting for your in-breath to begin on its own before raising your arms. As you experiment in this way, stay in touch with the sensation of your entire weight being supported by the earth. Do not let the movement of the arms, especially the movement upward, distract you from this ongoing sensation of support.

Now try this exact practice again, but this time also pay close attention to the movement of your breath during inhalation and exhalation. Notice how the gradual movement of the arms upward helps to open and fill the three basic breathing spaces—from the feet to the navel, from the navel to the middle of the chest, and from the middle of the chest to the top of the head. And the movement downward helps in the emptying process. Really pay attention to the spaciousness of the breath and how it seems to bring a sense of transparency and emptiness to your entire body as it is supported by the earth. Take several breaths in this way.

Now we're going to use sound to help release unnecessary tensions in the body and experience its inherent emptiness. Trying the same practice you just did, as you exhale while the arms are lowering, do so with the sound of "hummmm" through the entire exhalation. Whatever you do, do not push the humming sound to the very end, but let it subside when you still have a bit of air left in your lungs. At the end of the exhalation, wait for the next inhalation to take place through your nose. And then exhale with the "hummmm" again. Sense where the "hummmm" vibrates in your body—head, belly, chest, back, and so on. Sense how humming on the out-breath helps to release any tensions and blockages throughout your body. As your arms move downward, you may have a sense of energy also moving down from the top of your head to below your feet. Sense the deep inner silence and spaciousness at the very end of the exhalation as you wait for the new inhalation to arise on its own through your nose. Of course, as you practice being present in this way, stay in contact with the sensation of your weight being supported by the earth, since that is part of the reality of the present moment. Experiment with this practice daily for at least ten minutes until it becomes an integral part of your life.

Awakening to Who You Already Are

Perhaps the greatest Koan or riddle ever proposed is the heartfelt question, "Who am I?" Though our thoughts are always ready to answer this question, they fail in the face of the miracle of presence, of simple awareness of what is. But recognizing this miracle is seldom easy, especially for anyone caught up in thoughts and reactive emotions. It needs the support of the kind of practices given in this book. When we begin to pay attention to our breath in some of the many ways we have explored, however, and when our breath reveals the spaciousness that we are in our essence, we are no longer so much at the mercy of our habitual thoughts and emotions. We are no longer so easily able to lose our awareness of ourselves in them. We begin to *remember* the mystery of awakeness in this very moment. We see that we are not just what we are aware of—our bodies, emotions, thoughts, traumas, perceptions, and stories—but, perhaps more importantly, we are also the awakeness that reveals all of these *contents of experience*. There is no need to call this awakeness a Self or a non-Self. The awakeness simply is, and it is what illuminates our lives.

Check in on your breathing now. If you have worked with all the practices given in this book, this "checking in" will no doubt

114

Breathe into Being

be instantaneous and effortless. As you follow your breathing and watch what is happening within, you will realize that you in your essence are not your body, emotions, or thoughts, but that all of these are contained within the awakeness that is now present. Allow yourself to be called home to this awakeness and simply be what you already are. Whatever is happening, is happening. Whatever thoughts or feelings are revealed, they are just exactly what they are—neither more nor less. Though they are only fragments of your wholeness, most of which remains unseen, they are what you are faced with at this moment. They certainly do not define you in any final way.

There is no need for any kind of suggestion about how long you should work in this way. Being called home to the spacious wholeness of *now* has no time limits. It is where you have always been, though you may not have realized it.

115

Quest Books

encourages open-minded inquiry into
world religions, philosophy, science, and the arts
in order to understand the wisdom of the ages,
respect the unity of all life, and help people explore
individual spiritual self-transformation.
Its publications are generously supported by
The Kern Foundation,
a trust committed to Theosophical education.
Quest Books is the imprint of
the Theosophical Publishing House,
a division of the Theosophical Society in America.
For information about programs, literature,
on-line study, membership benefits, and international centers,
see www.theosophical.org
or call 800-669-1571 or (outside the U.S.) 630-668-1571.

Related Quest Titles

A long-time-student of Taoism, Advaita, and the Gurdjieff Work, Dennis Lewis teaches the transformative power of presence through Authentic Breathing®, qigong, meditation, and self-inquiry. He leads workshops throughout the United States at venues such as Esalen Institute, The New York Open Center, The Kripalu Center for Yoga and Health, and various qigong conferences.

His Taoist and qigong teachers include Mantak Chia, Dr. Wang Shan Long, and Bruce Frantzis. In the Gurdjieff Work his main teacher for fifteen years was John Pentland, who led the main line of the Work in America for many years. Lewis also had the good fortune to study for three years with Advaita Vedanta master Jean Klein.

His writing has appeared in numerous publications, including *Yoga Journal, Gnosis, Parabola, Somatics, Library Journal, Manas,* and the *San Francisco Chronicle.* He has been quoted in various books on qigong, Taoism, stress relief, and alternative medicine.

Lewis is the coeditor, with Jacob Needleman, of two books: *Sacred Tradition and Present Need* (Viking) and *On the Way to Self Knowledge* (Knopf). His book *The Tao of Natural Breathing: For Health, Well-Being and Inner Growth* was first published in September 1996 and was republished by Rodmell Press in May 2006. His two-cassette audio program entitled *Breathing as a Metaphor for Living* was released by Sounds True in September 1998, and then re-released on CD in April 2005 as *Natural Breathing.* His last book, *Free Your Breath, Free Your Life: How Conscious Breathing Can Relieve Stress, Increase Vitality, and Help You Live More Fully,* was published by Shambhala Publications in May 2004.

Lewis is a member of the National Qigong Association and is listed in *Who's Who in America.* He can be reached through his website: www.dennislewis.org.

MORE PRAISE FOR DENNIS LEWIS'S
Breathe into Being

"Dennis is a master teacher who stands fast in the profound truth that when we welcome this moment just as it is, life works. How astonishing and wonderful. The secret he reveals is that all that we need do is attend to our body's natural function of breathing in and breathing out. Nothing more is needed. Listen to Dennis. Be still and awaken into living your alive, joyful, and harmonious Presence that he so beautifully reveals."

—Richard Miller, Ph.D., author of *Yoga Nidra*: *The Meditative Heart of Yoga*, is cofounder of the International Association of Yoga Therapists

"*Breathe into Being* is both a fun and a must read. It is a fountain of practical wisdom for self-exploration and a most important self-help book, in the deeper sense of that expression."

—Glenn H. Mullin, author of *The Fourteen Dalai Lamas*: *A Sacred Legacy of Reincarnation*

"*Breathe into Being* is a practical yet profound guide to awakening, with simple exercises that allow one's inner light to shine forth. I highly recommend it."

—Leonard Laskow, M.D., author of *Healing with Love*